Afterlife

a new play by Michael Frayn

The world premiere of Michael F[...] National Theatre, following the acclaimed *Copenhagen* and *Democracy*. Roger Allam plays the great impresario Max Reinhardt.

FROM 3 JUNE • 020 7452 3000 No booking fee

nationaltheatre.org.uk

GRANTA

12 Addison Avenue, London W11 4QR
email editorial@granta.com
To subscribe go to www.granta.com or call 020 8955 7011

ISSUE 102

Shortlisted for the Orange Broadband Award for New Writers 2008

The
Voluptuous
Delights of
Peanut Butter
and Jam

Lauren Liebenberg

'Excellent and unsettling … Lauren Liebenberg grew up in Rhodesia, and it's clear that this, her debut novel, is drawn from her experience – a book that burrows deep under your skin'
Guardian

'This is an outstanding first novel about a little-chronicled period in history'
Mail on Sunday

virago.co.uk

CONTENTS

The new nature writing

When I used to think of nature writing, or indeed the nature writer, I would picture a certain kind of man, and it would always be a man: bearded, badly dressed, ascetic, misanthropic. He would often be alone on some blasted moor, with a notebook in one hand and binoculars in the other, seeking meaning and purpose through a larger communion with nature: a loner and an outcast. One such man was Christopher Johnson McCandless, a young educated American from a prosperous middle-class family who, in search of authenticity of experience and influenced by the writings of Tolstoy and Henry David Thoreau, dropped out from conventional society in the late 1980s to pursue a life of aimless wandering in the wild places of America. McCandless was disgusted by the excesses of our culture and by how in our rapacity and greed and arrogance we had, in his view, sought to separate ourselves from nature, had tried to place ourselves somehow outside or above it, so as to master it. In April 1992 he headed north to Alaska, because, he wrote in a letter, he wanted to 'walk into the wild'. He ended up starving to death; his decomposed body was found in a long-abandoned bus. He had hoped his encounter with the wilderness of the Alaskan taiga would heal his wounds: instead, they were ripped open.

I first read about McCandless in a 1993 article by Jon Krakauer in *Outside* magazine. It was at about this time that I also read Barry Lopez's *Arctic Dreams*(1986), a book that fundamentally changed the way I thought about nature and nature writing. For Lopez,

writing about the North American Arctic was not an exercise
in self-enthronement; he was not, like McCandless, a romantic
adventurer and wilderness was not a screen on to which he wanted
to project his longings and needs. As a field biologist he was
engaged in nothing less than a struggle for exactitude: the struggle
to find a language, free from cliché, in which to describe and
explain in all its complicated particularity a landscape undergoing
irrevocable change. It was a moral enterprise: for Lopez, the
wilderness of the Arctic was not a means to an end, a trove of
oil and gas for Arctic nations to exploit, but an end in itself. He
moved through this landscape with wonder, but also with care.

Lopez's book was not one of the many found among
McCandless's possessions after his death. Nor is there any record
of his having read it. If he had, his veneration of nature and in
particular of the Alaskan wilderness may have been tempered by
pragmatism, and he may not have lost his life.

Krakauer later expanded his article about McCandless into
a book, *Into the Wild*, which in turn has been adapted into a film.
'Into the Wild' would also do as a more general title for much of the
work being produced by a new generation of British nature writers,
preoccupied by McCandless's anxieties but balanced by Lopez's
methods. They share a sense that we are devouring our world, that
there is simply no longer any natural landscape or ecosystem that
is unchanged by humans. But they don't simply want to walk into
the wild, to rhapsodize and commune: they aspire to see with a
scientific eye and write with literary effect.

Few would doubt that we are living at a time of emergency. The
world's population presently stands at 6.7 billion, according to the
United Nations Department of Economic and Social Affairs. That
figure is projected to rise to 8.5 billion by 2030. It is understood
now just how quickly the earth is warming, because of the increase

in the atmospheric concentration of greenhouse gases arising from human activity. If the earth continues to warm at its present rate, we know what our fate will be, and yet we seem set on destroying ourselves. Meanwhile, we are experiencing a fundamental shift in power away from the West; the emergence of China, India and Brazil, with their new wealth and aspirational middle classes, is putting an intolerable strain on the world's finite resources. As I write the price of oil has reached $128 a barrel. It has never been higher. One need not be a pessimist to predict some kind of Malthusian denouement to the human story if we are unable or unwilling to alter our ways of being: scarcity wars, famine, large-scale environmental degradation.

When we began to commission articles for this issue we were interested less in what might be called old nature writing – by which I mean the lyrical pastoral tradition of the romantic wanderer – than in writers who approached their subject in heterodox and experimental ways. We also wanted the contributions to be voice-driven, narratives told in the first person, for the writer to be present in the story, if sometimes only bashfully. The best new nature writing is also an experiment in forms: the field report, the essay, the memoir, the travelogue. If travel writing can often seem like a debased and exhausted genre, nature writing is its opposite: something urgent, vital and alert to the defining particulars of our times.

The writers collected here are all on some kind of journey of discovery, as the best travel writers were, but at a time when so many of us are concerned about the size of our carbon footprint, they have no need to travel to the other side of the world to understand more about themselves and their relation to the world they inhabit. In this sense, many of the stories in this issue are studies in the local or the parochial: they are about the discovery of exoticism in the familiar, the extraordinary in the ordinary. They are about new ways of seeing. Many of the pieces can also be read as elegies: we know how our world is changing and what is being lost and yet we are powerless to prevent the change.

One of my favourite books about nature is not by a conventional nature writer at all: it is Erich Maria Remarque's *All Quiet on the Western Front*. The narrator is a young German conscript who spends several harrowing years in the trenches. Towards the end we encounter him sitting alone in a garden during two weeks away from the ceaseless slaughter: 'I have swallowed a bit of gas,' he confides. It is autumn 1918 and everyone 'talks of peace and armistice'. The garden is quiet, and he sits all day long in the sunshine, 'the trees show gay and golden, the berries of the rowan stand red among the leaves, country roads run white out to the sky.'

The years of fighting, of being surrounded by so much dirt, suffering and cruelty, have left the young man with an awareness of how disconnected he has become from the natural non-human world and from his fellow species. On the final page, shortly after he has returned to the front and with the end of the war so near, he is killed on a day of unusual quiet and stillness. In the film of the novel this last scene is reimagined so that a sniper shoots the young man just as he leans out of the trench, risking his life, to touch a butterfly that has landed nearby, beyond reach. The beauty and freedom of the butterfly is contrasted with the ugliness of war and the captivity of the soldier in his trench. War is an unnatural violation; there is the human world, the novel seems to be saying, and there is the natural world, and there is no longer any connecting bridge between them.

I was reminded of the final scene of the film of *All Quiet on the Western Front* – of a young man at war losing his life as he reaches for a butterfly – when I spoke to Lydia Peelle after reading her story 'Phantom Pain'. Peelle is a writer new to *Granta* and 'Phantom Pain' is the only work of fiction in this issue. 'The new nature writing,' she told me, 'rather than being pastoral or descriptive or simply a natural history essay, has got to be couched in stories – whether fiction or non-fiction – where we as humans are present. Not only as observers, but as intrinsic elements. I feel this is important, because we've got to reconnect ourselves to our environment and fellow species in every way we can, every chance we have. In my thinking, it is the tradition of the false notion of separation that has caused us so many problems and led to so much environmental degradation. I believe that it is our great challenge in the twenty-first century to remake the connection. I think our lives depend on it.'

This issue of *Granta* is our modest attempt to contribute towards that long journey of reconnection. At present, the human animal lives in but often strives to be apart from nature. None of us wishes to imagine what might come after nature, when we are gone. ■

Butterflies on a wheel

Between 1995 and 2005, because of graduate school, jobs, wanderlust and love, I moved across America sixteen times. Always by car, always in spring or fall. The drive I made most often was a 2,000-mile stretch between Idaho and Ohio, in either direction, sometimes alone, sometimes with my dog, once with a goldfish named Fran riding shotgun in a one-gallon water jug. Eastward, westward, I travelled the great unspooling latticework of American interstates – sun-baked juniper flats of southern Idaho, incandescent canyons of Utah, rambling prairies of Nebraska, the deep, heavy damp of Iowa in August.

It was on such a drive that I encountered one of the most marvellous things I've ever seen. I was crossing the western half of Wyoming, my car shuddering in a crosswind, big rafts of cumuli cruising above the highway. Everything seemed stripped clean by the wind and light. There was hardly any traffic, only a long-hauler now and then. Up ahead, the air grew abruptly darker, a thick band of grey, as if a long, opaque ribbon was being pulled along above the road. Within a few seconds, butterflies were exploding across the windshield. The air was thick with them: they cartwheeled over the hood; pieces of their wings lodged and vibrated in the wipers. For maybe a minute, at sixty then fifty then forty miles an hour, this kept up, thousands of butterflies breaking over the front of my Subaru. Sometimes their bodies seemed to simply pulverize – as if there were no liquid element to the creatures at all, just a wash of grey powder across the glass.

I decelerated to thirty, to twenty. When I was finally through the band, I pulled on to the shoulder, got out and walked back up the highway. I was maybe 1,000 miles from where I had started the day before and nearing that shaky, long-distance daze I would sometimes slip into, when I'd feel as though my brain was trailing way behind my body.

Butterflies: a long, shimmering curtain. Millions of them. They practically blotted out the sky. I felt as if some secret had torn free from the earth, something very private and old, something much larger than myself. I'd had feelings like this once or twice before: in the water off south-east Alaska, watching the wide, impossibly long silhouette of a humpback whale flow beneath my kayak; another time in the Gulf of California, watching a fisherman reach over the stern of a boat and seize the thrashing bill of a marlin with a gloved hand, and feeling in my bare feet the sleek, hard flank of the fish striking the underside of the boat. These were feelings that seemed to suggest the world possessed quantities of power I would never understand.

The butterflies coursed on and on. Some landed on fence posts, on the asphalt, on the roof of my car. A few landed on my sleeve and beat their wings carefully, thoughtfully, their bodies seeming to quiver in the wind.

Every now and then an eighteen-wheeler barrelled past, its wipers smearing back and forth, and a wreckage of insects tumbling in its wake. I stood on the shoulder of Interstate 80 for maybe fifteen minutes, waiting for the tail end of the swarm, staring up into a river of insects; staring up into the limits of my own understanding.

Some butterflies, I'd read later, migrate thousands of miles every year. In the fall, nearly every monarch butterfly in the United States east of the Rockies will attempt to fly to central Mexico.

After particularly rainy winters, painted lady butterflies migrate in the other direction, from Mexico into California, in their billions.

Salmon, wildebeest, locusts. Storks, swifts, snow geese. What if the torrents of animals migrating past us every year left behind traces of their routes? What if Arctic terns sketched lines through the sky as they poured out of Antarctica and back; what if steelhead trout left thin, colourful filaments behind as they muscled up our rivers? The skies above our fields would become a loom; the continents would be bundled in thread.

This year, as the leaves of spring unfurl, it's as if I can feel the energy pumping through the interior of my cells, mitochondria careering around, charged ions bouncing off membranes, everything arranging and rearranging, some ancient physiological dictate sending its psychotropic messengers galloping through my nervous system: sell the furniture, scrub out the refrigerator, call in sick.

The brain contains, always, two opposing desires: the urge to stay and the urge to run. One hour our house feels peaceful and snug; the next, I'm yanking open windows at two in the morning with my heart thudding against the darkness. Sixteen trips across the United States, a windshield grimed with heat and fingerprints, a grille caked with dust and insects, and I still think about those butterflies, resting for a moment on my sleeve, a ten-second lull in a merciless journey. ■

When the world turns ugly

Arguing with global warming sceptics over the years, I have noticed an interesting evolution in their case. First, I heard that no warming was taking place. Then I heard from them that yes, there might be warming after all, but that it was not caused by human activity. Then I heard that yes, there might be global warming, and yes, it might be caused by human activity, but that its effects, on the whole, will actually benefit humanity. Sure, global warming might result in a bit of severe drought here and there, along with rising sea levels, more destructive hurricanes and the extinction of species. But it will be good for American retirees, allowing them to stay in Minnesota for the winter rather than having to travel all the way to Florida. It will open up the Northwest Passage to shipping. Canada will become the world's hot new wine region.

Cost-benefit analysis is a tricky business, mixing, as it does, empirical science with individual values. If your preferences are weird enough, you might actually enjoy living in a world where the average temperature is a few degrees higher than it is today. (As David Hume remarked, ' 'Tis not contrary to reason to prefer the destruction of the world to the scratching of my finger.') Yet there is one point of view from which global warming is incontestably bad: the aesthetic point of view. A warming planet is a planet that's getting uglier. I'm not talking about the beauty of polar ice caps or coral reefs, but something more abstract and profound, something that goes right to the very nature of life and its relation to the rest of the universe.

What exactly do we get from the sun? Ask most people and they'll probably say 'heat' or 'energy'. But this is inaccurate. It's not really energy (of which temperature is a measure) that the earth has been amassing from the sun these five billion or so years. What terrestrial nature actually sucks out of the sky is order; or, to put it more abstractly, information. Properly viewed, global warming is a build-up of disorder – of information-destroying 'noise'.

The realization that nature imports order rather than energy from the sky is a relatively new one. In 1944, the Austrian theoretical physicist Erwin Schrödinger wrote a little book called *What is Life?* A couple of decades earlier, he had discovered the famous Schrödinger equation, the key to the new quantum theory. Now, as the heroic age of physics was giving way to that of molecular biology, he focused his attention on life.

Living things are made of matter, Schrödinger observed, yet they seem to violate the laws of physics. One of the most basic of these laws is the second law of thermodynamics, a universal tendency towards disorder. Entropy – a mathematical measure of the disorder present in a system – is always on the rise. Left on their own, things fall apart, run down, become inert; they tend towards an equilibrial state of chaos and dissolution. This is a matter of cruel probability: as we all know from our own domestic lives, there are vastly more ways for things to be disordered than to be ordered, so it is far more likely that things will slip from orderly to disorderly rather than the reverse.

But living things seem to buck this trend towards chaos. They 'keep going' much longer than inanimate things, putting off the moment when they reach that dangerous state of disorder known as death. How, Schrödinger asked, do living things cheat the second law of thermodynamics? Well, the second law says that entropy always increases in any system that is left alone; that is isolated from outside influences – the universe as a whole, for example. But living things are not isolated. They are always exchanging stuff with their environment. (Indeed, the German word for metabolism is *Stoffwechsel* – 'stuff exchange'.) What is this stuff? It's not matter: unless you are a child who is growing or an adult who is getting fat, your material content stays the same over time. It's not energy, either. True, animals do use up some energy moving around (unlike plants), but most of the energy we take in is radiated back into the environment in the form of heat. The crucial stuff – Schrödinger concluded – that a living thing absorbs from its environment is order.

Animals eat food containing highly ordered organic compounds and then return the material back to the environment as disordered waste (not entirely disordered: it's still of some value as manure). By feeding upon order, we offset our body's internal tendency towards greater entropy. We get these highly ordered organic compounds from green plants, which assemble them from (less ordered) water and carbon dioxide through the process of photosynthesis. Thanks to their chloroplasts, green plants are able to absorb what Schrödinger called 'negative entropy' from sunlight and fix it in material form.

Why, though, should the sun be a source of orderliness? Schrödinger did not say. But you can get a clue by going outside on a clear day and looking up. The sky is quite neat. It's nicely organized into a bright little disc surrounded by a lot of blue. If the sun were messily spread out over the entire sky, daytime and night-time, it would be useless to life on earth. Because of this orderliness, the sky is our friend in the struggle against entropy.

Terrestrial nature drinks up the sky's orderliness in a beautifully simple way. During the day, the earth gets energy from the sun in

the form of photons of visible light. At night, the same amount
of energy is dumped back out into space in the form of infrared
photons, otherwise known as radiant heat. Taken individually,
visible-light photons are more energetic than infrared photons.
(The energy of a photon is determined by its wavelength: the
shorter the wavelength, the higher the energy.) So, if the total
incoming/outgoing energy is to balance, there must be many more
energy-poor photons leaving at night than energy-rich photons
arriving by day. The key point is that more means messier. (In
technical language, each photon represents a 'degree of freedom',
and the more degrees of freedom, the greater the entropy.) The
energy the earth dumps back into space at night is less ordered
than the energy it receives from the sun during the day – just as
the waste animals excrete is less ordered than the foodstuffs they
eat. While there is a net gain in order, which sustains terrestrial life
in its struggle against entropy, there is no net gain in energy.

Or so we hope. Greenhouse gases trap the waste energy that
should be dumped into space. They keep the biosphere from
excreting disorder. Toxic entropy is building up. A warming
planet is not a more energetic planet, it's a more costive planet.
It's a more common planet, probabilistically speaking. And, if you
are neoclassical in your aesthetics and prize order as the essence
of beauty, it's an uglier planet.

Disorder is the essence of global warming, just as order is the
essence of life. But a mystery remains: why should the sky be a net
source of order for terrestrial nature? It didn't start out orderly.
Astronomical observations over the last couple of decades have
given us a snapshot of the early universe as a diffuse chaos: plenty
of entropy, no information. Gradually, however, this mess began to
grow more organized, as bits of it clumped together to form stars
and galaxies. Information spontaneously appeared: a featureless

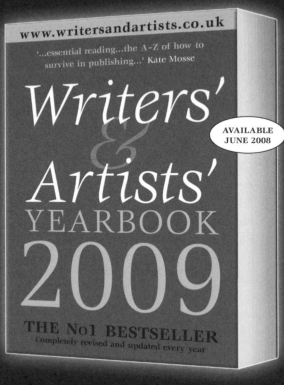
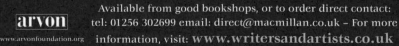

chaos is simple to describe, whereas a galaxy is complex. And the origin of the information must have been the gravity that caused the clumping. 'In some as yet ill-understood way,' the physicist Paul Davies has written, 'a huge amount of information evidently lies secreted in the smooth gravitational field of a featureless, uniform gas. As the system evolves, the gas comes out of equilibrium, and information flows from the gravitational field to the matter. Part of this information ends up in the genomes of organisms, as biological information.'

So the possibility of life was written into the gravitational field at the very origin of the universe. Somehow, the big bang was rather precisely organized. How precisely? The mathematical physicist Sir Roger Penrose has done the maths. To appreciate the odds against the early bang being smooth enough to give rise to a universe as rich in information as ours, you have to wrap your mind around this number: one, followed by a thousand trillion trillion trillion trillion trillion trillion trillion trillion trillion trillion zeros. (That's many more zeros than there are atoms in the universe.) In other words, for nature to be possible, the universe had to originate in a stupendously *unnatural* state. Otherwise it would have forever been a lifeless and chaotic wasteland. How to explain the fine-tuned smoothness? Three possibilities leap to mind. The first is that it was just wonderful dumb luck. The second is that God did it. The third is that physics will tell us once we finally arrive at a Final Theory that merges gravity, the theory of the big, with quantum mechanics, the theory of the small. My bet is on physics.

Meanwhile, perhaps we should do something about these greenhouse gases. The disorder is getting to be oppressive. ∎

The visions of Kurt Jackson

We face south-west towards the Isles of Scilly. To our left is a coastal hill, Carn Gloose. On our right is Cape Cornwall and beyond, exactly a mile offshore, I'm told, is a series of rocky outcrops known as the Brisons. In Priest's Cove we hop from boulder to boulder towards a series of larger, weed-mottled granite monoliths. They stand closer to the tide edge and offer us a perfect view of the incoming tide.

'Hear that?' he asks me as we search for a seat among the rocks. 'In the Cornish language it's called *mordros*. It's the only language, along with Greek and Polynesian, I think, that has a word for the sound of the sea.' Almost without pause, he continues. 'If you look at that line in the beach, you can see the exact place where the basaltic mudstones meet the granite.' Just these few details, like his translation of the Cornish place name (*carn* means 'rocky hillock' and *gloose* means 'grey-green') and his awareness of the precise distance the Brisons lie offshore, indicate a man deeply embedded in his landscape.

I'm with the artist Kurt Jackson who, after a childhood in which he regularly holidayed in Cornwall with his parents – both also painters – moved to England's most southerly county with his family in the early 1980s. Now in his late forties, he's regarded as one of the most important landscape artists in Britain. But the words 'landscape artist' don't really encompass the scope of his work. Some of his most glorious and ambitious paintings are of inner London and as far from the conventional notions of landscape as it's possible to be. Then there are the series of images depicting the lives of both Cornish charcoal makers and workers in the local slate quarry at Delabole. There was also his exhibition of works, completed deep inside the earth, on Cornwall's last working tin mines, or a parallel project in Iberia documenting Spanish and migrant Cornish miners.

There is an ecological relationship between Jackson and his paintings that makes them fascinating not merely to a lover of art, but also to a naturalist. It is in this second role, as a watcher of nature myself, that I've come to sit with Kurt Jackson over several days. My intention is to watch him as I might study a species of bird, like a rook or a jackdaw. The deep connection between Jackson's art and the landscape he occupies is my theme. It starts to unfold almost as we begin to settle into our pitch – opening the boxes of paints and crayons and adjusting our seats to observe our respective subjects. Suddenly, a small brown flake chips off the rocks ahead of us and acquires the power of flight. It performs a circuit around our heads and returns to its original perch. A high, clear, insistent alarm call, a sound that seems perfectly designed for puncturing the *mordros*, suggests that a type of small grey-brown bird called a rock pipit is alert to our arrival.

Jackson notes the presence of the pipit and explains how, sitting in the same spot for hours, such creatures often begin to accept him as a congenial part of the landscape. Birds and other animals – shrews, stoats, weasels – will come right up to him. Incidental details – minutely observed parts of the scene, perhaps the weather or the sounds he can hear, and very often the other species that share the habitat with him as he paints – will be noted in a little scribbled message on the canvas edge, and sometimes right across the top, through the sky. These marginal inscriptions often become the titles of his paintings.

Occasionally the signs he makes in this way are even more intimate. For some of the largest canvases, Jackson works barefoot, moving around them and even directly across them to apply the paint. On one huge piece I noticed a size-ten blue footprint. His paintings convey, even in the quiet and detachment of a gallery space, the pressing contingency of the places that inspire it, the unseen inhabitants to whom the landscape truly belongs, and the unseen artist who shared that moment with them.

If the incidental marks that he makes himself on the paintings are a form of personal signature to his work, then his borrowings from a place can seem like the landscape's own interventions. Wool is a favourite material, but you'll also find feathers and seaweed, leaves and twigs, even bits of sand and gravel out of a streambed. A recent memorable work documenting the River Avon is notable for the plastic bottles and other indestructible flotsam which have been engineered into the scene. But one of the most moving examples of Jackson's use of found materials is the way he experiments with mud that he collected from the shaft floor while working underground in a tin mine – the same dust that once blackened the faces and blighted the lungs of miners here in Cornwall and elsewhere. Dirt converted to art.

As we watch the Atlantic pounding in towards us, I find myself being distracted from the study of Jackson by another rare bird in the landscape. While the artist sketches out a preliminary scene, I spot a peregrine falcon – probably a male – as it cruises over the sea. A slate-grey bullet, it steers south and west but is blown gradually inland towards us. It rises over Carn Gloose and loiters, the air rinsing its wings, the bird wind-held. Jackson sees it with the naked eye as soon as it slips free of the Brisons. He then turns back to his work, as he pushes a fistful of brushes across his portrayal of the leaden sky from which the bird has just flown.

Immense elemental forces often seem to lie just below the surface of Jackson's paintings. There is also a sense of the earth-quaking energies that first initiated the proto-landscape from which the present scene evolved. When I see his works of Priest's Cove, for instance, I see not only the finished granite boulders, but I can *feel* the molten magma that gave them birth, awkwardly and violently, aeons ago.

As soon as I see that fistful of brushes scouring back and forth across the canvas, I begin to sense the answer is at hand. There is a frenetic pace to the way in which Jackson works: hands roving, sometimes as if panic-stricken, for pencils and bottles, inks and crayons. He then breaks off briefly to incise with a razor blade a bruised grey sky he has just laid down. The act of slashing vigorously at his own work makes me realize that the energies conveyed in the paintings are achieved by a gradual slackening of control over the forces that create them. This releasing of himself into the process reaches its climax about half an hour later, as the roar of the sea imposes its ineluctable rhythm on us both.

I'm struck most by the sheer range of materials and techniques: not just the spectrum of ink bottles, crayons, pastels, pencils – the material stuff he uses – but also odd things such as the moment when he grabs the actual palette itself, dragging it repeatedly over the layers of colour. Another time he empties the muddy water – which he's used earlier in mixing his colours – wholesale out of the palette on to the painting and starts working with that. The razor blade is deployed repeatedly, and if that doesn't create the desired effect, Jackson uses his nails and tells me that he never bites them precisely because of their instrumental value to him. At one point, in fact, he uses all ten fingers and thumbs and it looks as if he's playing the piano in his own wet paint.

On another occasion I can actually count the number of

brushes in his hand. He has twelve and wields them like a weapon against the image. Then he can hold them not by their handles, pencil-wise, but laid flat in the palm of his hand, with the bristles flicked almost individually so that tiny specks of paint are sprayed on to the painting. The subtlety of this last technique contrasts sharply with his method of swiping the brush hard at the picture, like a swordsman testing a blade, lacing the canvas with great big drops of paint. At the finish, he blows hard and stands back. The earlier crescendo has taken five minutes, but it feels like – in fact, you know that it is – the summation of twenty-five years of apprenticeship, a word he cherishes. I work out afterwards that he uses a different approach or technique every thirteen seconds, and at times I found it nearly impossible to observe him and write up the processes as they happened.

Improbably, given the intensity of his application both to the changing landscape and to the even faster-moving portrait of it, Jackson talks to me all the while. Or rather, I should say, he's talking to himself. But I do manage to capture the last word: 'MENTAL!' It's odd – given the ecstatic tumult of the preceding minutes – that it's not a reference to himself, or a comment even on how I might be feeling. He nods to the sea: 'Looks as if they're about to overwhelm you…the waves.'

There are two mental scenes before me. There is the Atlantic and the rock. And over Jackson's shoulder, I glimpse its twin: the painting of the grey-turquoise sea-slump, calm and expansive, just behind a frenzy of white spume careening into the basalt's blackness. It is the *mordros* made visible – a thing of colour and elemental contest and of beauty. ■

www.granta.com
See Kurt Jackson's paintings

Elegy

Just round a corner of the afternoon,
Your novel there beside you on the bed,
Your spectacles to mark your place, the sea
Just so before the tide falls back,
Your face will still be stern with sleep
As though the sea itself must satisfy
A final test before the long detention ends
And you can let the backwash take you out.
The tall green waves have waited in the bay
Since first you saw the water as a child,
Your hand inside your father's hand, your dark eyes
Promising you heartbreak even then.
Get on with it, I hear you say. *We've got no choice.*

We left the nursing home your tired chair.
They stole the sweets and flowers anyway
And bagged your clothes like rubbish in the hall.
Here in the flat your boxed-up books and ornaments
Forget themselves, as you did at the end.
The post still comes. The state that failed to keep the faith
Pursues you for its money back. *There's nothing worse,*
You used to say, *than scratting after coppers.*
Tell that to the clerks who'd rob your grave,
Who have no reason to remember how
You taught the children of the poor for forty years
Because it was the decent thing to do.

It seems there's no such thing as history.
We must have dreamed the world you've vanished from.
This elegy's a metaphysical excuse,
A sick-note meant to keep you back
A little longer, though you have no need to hear
What I must say, because your life was yours,
Mysterious and prized, a yard, a universe away.

But let me do it honour and repay your gift of words.
I think of how you stared into the bonfire
As we stood feeding it with leaves
In the November fog of 1959,
You in your old green coat, me watching you
As you gazed in upon
Another life, a riverside address
And several rooms to call your own,
Where you could read and think, and watch
The barges slip their moorings on the tide,
Or sketch the willows on the further shore,
Then in the evening stroll through Hammersmith
To dances at the Palais. *Life enough*,
You might have said. *An elegant sufficiency.*
There was a book you always meant to write.

You turned aside and lit a cigarette.
The dark was in the orchard now, scarf-soaking fog
Among the fallen fruit. The house was far away,
One window lit, and soon we must go back
For the interrogation to begin,
The violence and sorrow of the facts
As my mad father sometimes dreamed they were
And made the little room no place at all
Until the fit was past and terrible remorse
Took hold, and this was all the life we had.

To make the best of things. Not to give up.
To be the counsellor of others when
Their husbands died or beat them. *To go on.*

I see you reading, unimpressed, relentless,
Gollancz crime, green Penguins, too exhausted
For the literature you loved, but holding on.
There was a book you always meant to write,
In London, where you always meant to live.
I'd rather stand, but thank you all the same, she said,
A woman on the bus to Hammersmith, to whom
I tried to give my seat, a woman of your age,
Your war, your work. We shared the view
Of willowed levels, water and the northern shore
You would have made your landing-place.
We haven't come this far to give up now.

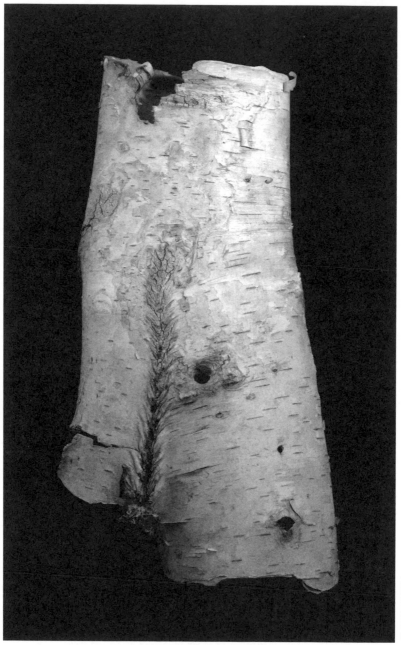

The whisper of love

In Antonio del Pollaiuolo's picture of Apollo and Daphne in the National Gallery in London, the god appears like a bare-legged teenage sprinter who has just managed to lay hands on the fleeing nymph. Myth requires her to take root on the spot and begin to sprout laurel leaves and branches, so her loosely robed left leg does appear to be grounded while two big encumbering bushes have sprung from stumps on her shoulders. But her face between the laurel boughs looks back without panic at the face of her pursuer, just as the inside of his left thigh is making contact with the bare calf of her right. Intact she may be, but she remains forever touched and susceptible.

Laurel as emblem of a chaste escape makes sense, especially nowadays when the bush belongs so brightly and trimly in the domestic hedge. Daphne's two sky-besoms do signify her joy at being out of reach, but a part of her is still reluctant to be free, the part suggested by bare legs at full tilt, the part where the erotic vies with the ethereal, the part that is more a birch tree than a laurel.

Birch is the tree of desire, ashimmer with sexual possibility even when it arrives swathed in botanical Latin. *Betula pendula* and *betula pubescens*, names of the silver and the downy birch, have an indolent sensual loll to them; and technical descriptions of their various characteristics are equally suggestive, the silver variety having 'young twigs hairless, with white warts', the downy having 'young twigs with velvety white hairs, without warts'. No wonder the tree reminded the poet Louis Simpson of 'a room filled with breathing, / The sway and whisper of love', where arms being raised to unclasp an earring are like a sallow trunk dividing into pale, smooth, slender branches.

Simpson's birch is warmly and consentingly adult, as if it were a grown-up member of the group Robert Frost saw once after an ice-storm in a New England wood, bowed down like girls on their hands and knees, throwing their hair 'before them over their heads to dry in the sun'. And the first time I entered a New England wood I too was full of the stir of poetry, and much else besides. I had read in Robert Graves's *The White Goddess* that *beith*/birch was the synonym for B in the Ogham alphabet, and had translated Mad Sweeney's praise of the trees of Ireland, where the blessed, smooth-skinned *beithe bláith bennachtach* sways magically in the breeze, under its crown of plaited twigs. But there and then all that airy, erotic energy and association got captured and confined (much as Ariel was by Sycorax in a cloven pine) in a section of birch trunk I found on the wood floor.

This was a thick-stemmed piece of sapling about ten inches long and as thick as a nymph's leg above the ankle, in the shape of a Y that had been pruned. Just above where the young trunk divided, the two branches had snapped off, and afterwards the thing lay marinating in a compost of old leaves and moss until the heartwood turned altogether soggy. When I discovered it, the innards had actually decayed to the point where I was able to clear out the mush and was left holding an open-ended sheath of bark, flecked and grained, warted, dampish, a little bit tufty-downy at the cleft.

This was in May 1979, beside Eagle Pond in New Hampshire, where I had gone with my family to visit the poet Donald Hall, friend of Louis Simpson, disciple of Frost, and the inheritor of his grandfather's farm, to which he had only recently returned. Eventually, therefore, my chance find became a memento of our visit to his poetry station, the memento became a keepsake, and when I read that the birch is 'a light-demanding tree and will not grow in the shade of others', the keepsake began to shine in my mind like a Platonic idea.

At the end of the weekend I took it back to Harvard and have not parted with it since. First I let it dry (when it stiffened, it was as if the word 'birch' were turning into the older 'birk'); then I stood the blunted Y shape upside down so that it became a little torso agleam in its own whiteness, a *puella* forever *pubescens*, an armless, legless Venus de New Hampshire, as disinclined to move as Daphne was desperate to flee. A form which seems to ponder Rilke's response to the archaic torso of Apollo – 'You must change your life' – before answering wistfully, 'Yes, perhaps, but first you have to live it.' ∎

Helicobacter pylori bacteria grazing in the stomach

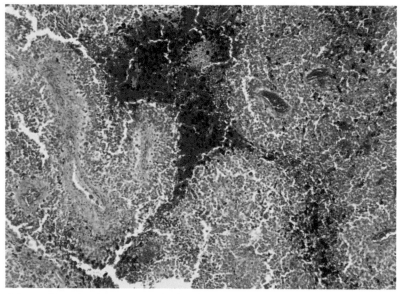

A human liver showing a metastasized melanosarcoma

PATHOLOGIES

A startling tour of our bodies

Kathleen Jamie

A few hours before my mother died, eventually of pneumonia, the disease they call 'the old man's friend', in a small side room with muted lighting in our local hospital, there was a deluge of rain. I can't recall whether curtains or a blind screened the window, but I remember being puzzled by the sudden hissing noise, and crossing the room to peer outside, and seeing flat roofs, and the sheeting rain in the October night.

The sound of the rain, and of my mother's breathing. It was about three a.m. There would be no more medical interventions. Nature would be 'allowed to take its course'.

The days following such a death, when death is a release rather than a disaster, have a high, glassy feel, as though a note was being sung just too high to hear. It was a strange hiatus, all appointments cancelled. Between the death and the funeral, the phone calls and the arrangements, between the time spent with my father and sister, and my brother's arrival home from abroad, I went out walking on the hills behind town. The hillsides give views of the estuary below, then the land rising again on the river's north bank. The sky and river were beautiful and glassy, as though they were the source of that high-sung note. Nature was back in her accustomed place: outdoors, in the trees' colours, in the tidal flux of the river, in the fieldfares arriving in the fields. I often thought about the phrase 'letting nature take its course' and how it sounded like a gallantry, how it suggested humility and timeliness.

About a month later, and further north, there was a one-day conference, which was about humanity's relationship with other species. It was an impassioned affair. A government minister began the day, then a climate scientist gave dire warnings, then came writers and activists, all speaking with urgency about how we have to 'reconnect with nature'. We have a crisis because we have lost our ability to see the natural world, or find it meaningful. There had been a breakdown in reciprocity. Humanity had taken a wrong path, had become destructive and insulated.

The guests spoke from a raised podium with a nineteenth-century stained-glass window behind. Through the window, we, the audience, could see an occasional herring gull glide by, coloured red by the glass. A lunch of local venison was served, then came the afternoon's speakers, who suggested that consumerism was a poor substitute for wonder. One told a gripping story about an encounter with sea lions, another about a transforming experience with polar bears. It was dramatic in itself, but, he suggested, it carried wider meanings about our relationship with other creatures.

It was wearing on for Christmas. Outside the conference venue the streets were filled with shoppers, and the stained-glass window darkened early. Perhaps I was still tired from my mother's death, thin-skinned and bad-tempered, but when the day ended with time for questions, I had some turning in my head, though I didn't raise my hand. Questions about 'nature' mostly, which we were exhorted to embrace. What was it exactly, and where did it reside? I'd felt *something* at my mother's bedside, almost an animal presence. The old man's friend is admitted, but what about when he comes for the children? What are vaccinations for, if not to make a formal disconnection from some of these wondrous other species? And what did we just eat, vegetarians aside? Deer meat, and very nice too.

The train home was busy and it broke down briefly, but people were good-natured considering we were packed close to each other in a metal box. We were out on a dark Highland moor, but the last wolf had been shot long ago.

In the new year I wrote to Professor Frank Carey, clinical consultant in pathology at Ninewells Hospital in Dundee. I'd met Frank before and knew him as a level-headed and considerate man, tall, with a soft Irish accent, and a good teacher. We were at a similar age and stage in life, with growing children and parents beginning to succumb. If he thought my request was prurient, he didn't say so. Rather, he and his colleagues seemed glad of outside interest in their speciality. Usually people shy away.

I told Frank about the environmentalists' and writers' conference, and how the foreshortened definition of 'nature' was troubling me. I'd come home grumpy, thinking, 'It's not all primroses and dolphins.' There's our own intimate, inner natural world, the body's weird shapes and forms, and sometimes they go awry. There are other species, not dolphins arching clear from the water, but bacteria that can pull the rug from under us. I asked, 'Please show me what's going on.'

I was gabbling all this as we walked down the gleaming hospital corridors one February morning. Frank reached out to open yet another double door, saying, 'You know, till now, I'd never really thought of it as "nature".' I wondered, as I had at my mother's bedside, and the conference, if there was a distinction somewhere I had simply failed to understand.

If pathologists are seen as slightly sinister, it's because they're the ones conducting urgent post-mortems in TV detective dramas. But the architecture doesn't help. The pathology labs were inevitably downstairs, in the lower reaches, the bowels of the building. Their main doors were protected by keypads and a sign announced fiercely that the department was UNDER 24-HOUR LOCKDOWN. But I was there now. In his small office, Frank found a white lab coat for me, the first time I'd ever worn such a thing, the attire of the scientist, and suggested we start with surgical specimens, in the 'cut-up room'. The cut-up room. I drew breath, but after my mother's death, and all the gentle euphemisms, and that conference, with its reverent talk of far-off polar bears and 'transforming experiences', I was actually quite glad to have arrived at a place where a spade was called a spade. Frank said, 'Are you squeamish?'

The door opened to a soft roar, the ventilation system. The wall opposite the door was all windows, but white blinds were drawn and electric lights switched on. Tall shelving units held plastic trays and little tubs and boxes, and there were three or four long workbenches. At intervals on the workbenches lay green plastic chopping blocks. Other people, also in white coats, were already at work, standing at the benches, attending to things I couldn't see. I swore I would use no food similes, no culinary imagery at all, but of course it looked like a school cookery classroom, or 'domestic science' as they were pleased to call it then. The atmosphere was serious, but convivial.

Professor Carey led me to his place, then brought a tray of instruments. These he put to the left of the green block. To its right was a sink. In the tray were long tweezers and blunt-ended scissors. He spent a minute fixing a shining, newly sterilized blade on to a handle. Then he went off and at once returned with a grey plastic tub big enough to need carrying in both hands. He opened it and poured into the sink a gallon of liquid.

'Formaldehyde,' he said.

'It doesn't smell...'

'It's the ventilation. There's a very strong downdraught. Formaldehyde is pretty toxic, it wouldn't do to breathe it or get it on your skin.'

Then he grasped the object inside the tub and laid it on the chopping block. It was a drowned-looking thing, obviously of the body, big enough to be alarming: about ten inches long, rubbery brownish-pink, with an entourage of fattiness and membranes. I didn't know what I was looking at, but Frank soon told me it was someone's colon, or part of one, about a third. A colon is a tube, as you'd suppose, but the surgeon who'd removed it had sealed the lower end, the rectum end, with metal staples and that end was about the size of a child's fist. The upper ten inches had been sliced open, revealing the inner surface. This surface was pale yellow-brown, and ribbed like a beach at low tide. It was a natural artefact all right, but far from elegant, and if I hadn't been told I couldn't have said whether it belonged to an aquarium, a puppet theatre, or a bicycle repair shop.

'When was this taken out?'

Frank glanced at the notes. 'Two days ago.'

'So the patient is still upstairs?'

'She will be, yes. Oh yes.'

Professor Carey began by turning the colon in his gloved hands, scrutinizing and assessing it. He would have to write a 'macro report' describing what he had, its dimensions and such, before it was sliced up. He stretched a piece of translucent membrane between three fingers to show me, and said complimentary things about the surgeon, a beautiful Iranian woman who was pointed out to me later. Her scalpel had carefully followed this membrane, releasing the colon from its context, bringing it to the outside world.

'The tumour's down here,' said Frank, pushing a gloved finger into the colon's lower end. He prodded around for a moment, then turned the colon inside out to show me a hard whitish deposit adhering to the inner wall. It seemed of no more consequence than chewing gum dropped on a pavement, but there it was.

The cutting followed a set procedure. Frank held the colon with one hand and with the long knife took parings from each end, the 'margins'. In due course, these would be examined microscopically. If the tumour was cancerous, and cancer cells were found within a millimetre of the margin, there was a chance that cancer cells remained in the patient's body. These things determined the course of treatment prescribed. He sliced the tumour itself into pieces not much bigger than a thumbnail and laid these in order at the top of his board. Then began the search for lymph nodes.

There's nothing dainty about the search for lymph nodes. If the cancer had spread from the original tumour, it would have done so via the lymph system. By examining these lymph nodes under the microscope Frank would be able to tell if it had travelled and how far. He began carving decisively through the whole colon. As each slice slumped from his blade he dragged it to a clear section of the board and began mashing the fatty surround against it with his fingertips. I watched as Frank worked, again trying to resist any food similes, but they would come. The pile of sliced colon mounting at the far edge of his board looked like chanterelle mushrooms, the fat squished under his fingers like cottage cheese. It might have been 'nature' but there was nothing uplifting about it. Well, we are predators and omnivores, we are meat and made of food, and the colon is part of how our animal bodies deal with food.

At one point Frank said, 'Amazing how much like animals we are. This could be a pig's colon. We occasionally get veterinary specimens in, just for interest.'

'It shouldn't really surprise us...'

'That we're like animals? No, it shouldn't. But it still does.'

Lymph nodes feel like lentils or grains of rice, so they resist being squashed. They are pale brown. As he found these auguries, he laid them out in order. They looked like a row of baby teeth, only more yellow. One was markedly bigger than the others, which was not a good sign.

When he was satisfied, he tipped the board and scraped the residue of the colon into a polythenc bag. The samples of margin and tumour and the lymph nodes went into tiny plastic boxes, ready to be mounted in wax, sliced, stained and prepared for the microscope. And that was that. One person's disaster, another's routine.

I kept having to do a mental exercise, every so often, to unhook myself from the colon being cut up in front of me, which was not a beautiful object of contemplation, and consider what it meant. To think upstairs, I mean, to that person lying ill and frightened and anxiously awaiting 'the results from the lab'. Other people in the room were working on lumps taken from breasts, an appendix. I'd said as much to Frank, about having to make an effort to empathize, and as he'd worked we'd talked of people we knew who'd had cancer, even in our own families. The sheer painful ghastly slog of it; the changed landscapes of a life, the unexpected declarations of love.

A couple of weeks passed before I could again go to the pathology labs; the snowdrops faded, the evening light lengthened. A neighbour asked if we could look after her son for the day, while she went to the funeral of a young colleague who'd died of cancer. This time Professor Carey suggested we look at the next stage, the histology, or examination of cells through the microscope. Today it was a liver.

The computer screen in his office was showing a substantial portion of one, with the gall bladder attached. The pictures had been taken after the liver was excised, but before cut-up. The severed edge, about three inches tall, had been cauterized and so was blackened slightly. Tiny threads hung down, where arteries had been tied off. They reminded me of rock climbers' gear, abandoned on a rock face.

It had been removed, like the colon, because of a tumour – a big one this time. It bulged out of the liver like a gloved fist.

Professor Carey pointed out these features with his pen, then said, 'Okay. Tell me if you feel seasick.'

This time he meant seasick, not squeamish. The microscope was a double-headed one which allowed us both to see the same slide, and for one unused to microscopes, it was like slipping into a dream. I was admitted to another world, where everything was pink. We were looking from a great height down at a pink river – rather, an estuary, with a north bank and a south. There were wing-shaped river islands and furthermore it was low tide, with sandbanks exposed. It was astonishing, a map of the familiar: it was our local river, as seen by a hawk.

'It's like the Tay!' I said. 'At low tide. With the sandbanks.'

'I love the names of those sandbanks...' said Professor Carey. 'Now, we should start with the normal and move to the abnormal... Let's look south.'

As though on a magic carpet we flew to the south side of the estuary and there Frank showed me how the arrangement of cells was ordered and calm. The sample had been stained with hematoxylin and eosin; organic, commonly used stains which show the nuclei and cytoplasm respectively. Frank could distinguish blues and purples; to my eye all was shades of pink, though I have a poor sense of colour. But it was a bright and pretty bird's-eye view of an ordered, if unusual, land. I saw trails of nuclei and the cells' supporting framework of reticulin. The reticulin looked a little like field dykes, the marks of a long inhabitation of the land. Here the cells were doing as nature intended, unconsciously getting on with tasks quotidian and wondrous: the filtering and clearing and storing and production.

'This is healthy tissue. Bear it in mind.'

Then we were swinging north, crossing the river, which was a vein rising into the liver from the intestine. On the river's north bank, we stopped and hovered over a different kind of place, densely packed, all dark dots that seemed too busy for comfort. Frank didn't have to tell me this was the tumour. Although it was also still, and fixed and a pretty colour, there was a chancy, frenetic feel to it. An arena with too many nuclei crammed together; as Frank pointed out, the 'architecture' was improper, the cells' structures and shapes were slewed, the supporting framework absent.

He said, 'The good thing is, these are still liver cells, they haven't been imported from a primary tumour somewhere else. They're still trying to behave like a liver, but...'

He looked quietly for a moment, then said, 'Cancer was named for the crab, because a cancer tumour sends claws out into the surrounding tissue. It's one thing we look for in arriving at a diagnosis of cancer, whether the tumour is self-contained, "encapsulated", or whether it's reaching out with claws. At cut-up I was happier because it seemed self-contained, but look...'

We swooped low, until we were above a feature that crooked from the shore into the river, a bit like a jetty. When the magnification increased, you could see this was also crowded, and made of the same dense tumour tissue. 'And there is also this.' Now he focused on one of those areas I'd so delightedly thought of as sandbanks, with their old, suddenly apposite Scots names: Reckit Lady, the Shair as Daith. There too, we looked down on the same kind of tissue.

'So we have some vascular invasion.'

Frank made a note, then said, 'We had a trainee for a while, and whenever she saw something like this, she'd say, "Aw, what a shame. What a *shame*." Now, let me show you something else.'

It all seemed like bad news but I leaned back into the microscope, to be guided by Frank's trained eye. In the healthy liver, he led me to two tiny dots and increased the magnification. The dots expanded into a double image, what looked like a pair of boxing hares.

'That's a cell dividing normally. The chromosomes are lined up equally. That cell has been arrested just at that moment in its cycle, this is *life*. But see here.'

Again we travelled north, over to the tumour, and within its mass Frank quickly found another dividing cell, but if they were two boxing hares, one hare was hugely bigger than the other, claiming strength and advantage. His report would call them 'abnormal mitotic figures' – cells dividing wrongly, and too many, and too fast.

I sat back and rubbed my eyes.

'So that's that?' I asked bleakly, meaning, that's going to kill him? The little hook out into the vein, the intimate, crowded island, a mere smear on a glass slide.

Frank sounded surprised. 'Not at all! He's in with a good chance. The tumour's been successfully removed, and you can't actually make definite predictions from what we've seen... He'll have chemotherapy. And the liver regenerates, you know. Though he's had that large section removed, it'll be growing back.'

As Frank put the slides away on a tray in their proper order I glanced about his office, resting my eyes. A couple of lab coats on a peg, books and files on a shelf, pathology textbooks, a child's drawing, a bicycle helmet, the window screened by a pale blind. 'Flying' may have been an illusion, but it was one my body believed, because I was feeling queasy, with all this swooping down and up. Queasy, but cheered.

'Would you like to see more? You said you were interested in infections, I set aside a couple of infections for you...'

'You're very kind.'

This time the country beneath was a gorgeous sapphire blue. It had a north-facing shoreline, and a mile or so inland, so to speak, were regularly spaced ovals, turned with the narrow end towards the coast. They might have been craters, or even sports stadiums. Frank was describing it to me with his customary quiet level-headedness. He was speaking of 'columnar structures' but it took me a while to understand that he meant the ovals; they were sections cut horizontally through columns. These were acid-producing glands; we were in the lining of someone's stomach.

Between the oval structures were valleys, if you like, fanning down to the shore. Frank wanted to show me something in one of these valleys and I couldn't find it at first, it took several patient attempts – this microscope didn't have a cursor device to point at things. It was a very human moment, a collusion of landscape and language when one person tries to guide the other's gaze across a vista. And what vistas! River deltas and marshes, peninsulas and atolls. The unseen landscapes within. Looking down a microscope you might imagine you were privy to the secrets of the universe, some Gaian union between body and earth, but I dare say it's to do with our eyes. Hunter-gatherers that we are, adapted to look out over savannahs, into valleys from hillsides. Scale up the absurdly small until it looks like landscape, then we can do business.

'There!' said Frank. 'Isn't that a pastoral scene? They're grazing!'

I had it: six or seven very dark oval dots, still tiny, despite the magnification, were ranged across the blue valley, like musk oxen on tundra, seen from far above.

'This is *Helicobacter pylori* – they're bacteria. They irritate the stomach, the stomach produces too much acid, and so they cause stomach ulcers. Obvious as anything now, but they just weren't seen till 1984. It was an Australian pathologist who spotted the association between inflamed stomachs and these things. He was a bit of a crazy. No one took him seriously, no one believed stomach ulcers could be caused by bacteria. But…he found another crazy to work with and together they got the Nobel Prize. Probably saved thousands and thousands of lives. The thing is, you perceive what you expect, what you're accustomed to. Sometimes it needs a fresh eye, or a looser mind…'

'You can die of stomach ulcers?'

'Yes. You bleed.'

'Grazing' was the word. Although the landscape was bright blue – a stain called Giemsa – it was an image you might find in a Sunday night wildlife documentary. Pastoral, but wild too. So close to home, but people had walked on the moon before these things were discovered, free in the wilderness of our stomachs.

'You wonder what their function is, their purpose…'

'No purpose. They're not conscious. They just are. These things have been co-evolving with us for millennia and millennia. They've adapted to live in acid. There are some people, you know, who take the stomach as evidence of "intelligent design", because it contains its own acid; you walk around with a bag of acid in you, and come to no harm. But it's evolved that way, and these things have evolved with it.'

'So what will happen?'

'A course of antibiotics should put paid to them.'

'And do you think there are other things, other associations, we're just not seeing?'

'Oh, certainly. Now, would you like to look at something else?'

Of course I did. More little journeys to strange new shores. The nature within. Nature we'd rather do without. If I were a pathologist, I think I ought always to have that woman in the room, the one who kept saying, 'Aw, what a *shame*', a one-woman Greek chorus, otherwise I fear I'd be seduced by the bright lights and jewel colours, the topography, flora and fauna, so caught up among the remote and neutral causes I'd forget the effects.

Again Frank swapped slides, and again the world was pink. We were in the small intestine and this time I had no trouble seeing the beast in question; it was cruising along the indentations of a coastline like a gunship. A pink triangular balloon, with a thin mean tail – though microscopic, it was big enough to be thuggish, and I said so.

'Ah, you see, you're personalizing it. It's just a one-celled organism, a protozoan.'

'Morally neutral.'

'Morally neutral. This is Giardia. You've been to Asia... You know, stomach cramps, constant diarrhoea? So debilitating. And chronic. It doesn't kill you, but it makes you very ill...it's endemic in Asia and Africa, but occasionally it turns up here, in wells and springs. Cattle get it too, and sheep and deer.'

He studied it for a moment, then leaned back from the microscope, saying with sudden feeling, 'This thing's a *pest*.'

Pestilence and disease. It's pretty grim. Who wants the privacy of their body invaded and bits cut out and chopped up and the remnants scraped into a polythene bag? But we'll go a long way not to die. Who wants their neighbour down the street or round the world to bleed into her stomach when a course of antibiotics will do the trick? We need disease to dance us on our way, we need to halt it if we're to live morally. Twin truths, like boxing hares.

I drove home along the river I'd fancied I'd seen in the poor man's liver cells. The tide was in, no sandbanks. The inner body, plumbing and landscapes and bacteria. The outer world had also flown open like a door, and I wondered as I drove what is it that we're *just not seeing*?

On my third visit Frank relayed an unsettling invitation. A colleague, Professor Stewart Fleming, whom I had met last time, was that morning conducting a post-mortem.

We looked at each other.

'Think about it,' said Frank.

I paused for a long moment, then asked, 'What do you think yourself?'

It was his turn to pause.

'Why don't we look in later, in a couple of hours, when he's finishing up, just for a minute or two?'

It lay on my mind. Why refuse? Because it felt scary, and like a transgression. My own motives may be impure: idle curiosity, a good dinner-party story. 'Guess what I did on Wednesday!' Why attend? Because...there were just some things to come to terms with.

A featureless door, guarded by a keypad. No signs, no notices declaring lockdowns, just a door in the wall. As Frank was tapping in the number, my heart lurched in fear of what it would open to reveal.

'What are we going into?'

'Sorry,' said Frank. 'Nothing, here.'

A narrow flight of stairs, leading, of course, down, and round a corner. At the bottom was another door. This one gave into a small hall, lined with white locker doors, with people's names handwritten in red pen. Corpses, waiting for the undertakers to arrive and discreetly take them away. A porter gave us a jolly hello as we passed and at a further corner Frank held out a staying hand, saying, 'Wait here a moment,' as he went ahead.

No doubt they were doing some tidying. Concealing this and washing that. I had no lab coat today, and felt suddenly wrongly dressed: it had all gone serious and I was in too bright a skirt, too casual a top. Everything around was clean and metallic. Then Frank reappeared, saying, 'You can come in now.'

The scene was composed like a painting, or a ritual: the living and the concealed dead. In a wide clean open space the body, shrouded in white, lay on a metal table to the left. At the back wall a figure in a green gown and hat glanced towards us then turned back to the sink where she was occupied. Above her were windows for observers. Professor Fleming, dressed in green scrubs, was pushing towards me a metal tray on wheels. I couldn't see what lay on the tray until we met, and I looked down. At that point he said, 'Okay?' I think he meant, you're not about to faint? It happens, sometimes.

'Okay,' I said.

He pointed. 'This is the heart, this is the left lung.'

With splayed fingers and a soft scraping motion he pulled the heart across the tray. It left a smear of blood.

'I've cut it open, see?'

Deftly – this was a substance he was used to handling – he began to fold the opened heart back into shape, like a small bag. The word 'cutpurse' came to mind, an old name for a thief. I nodded, and though I would have liked to have seen again how the heart was made, more slowly, it seemed improper to ask and already I was aware of the smell, fresh, rude, rising up and summoning some primal response I didn't really want to acknowledge.

I looked from the heart, the chubby texture of its walls, its inertness, up to Professor Fleming's eyes as he spoke, back down to the heart. The quick and the dead. I could sense, rather than see, the shrouded shape of the corpse.

The lung, smaller than you might imagine, had a smoother texture, but worked through its redness were threads of black.

'That's just carbon deposit. Every city-dweller has that in their lungs...'

Now the smell was insistent, a blood-red rose.

'And what...?' I asked.

'This...you'll have heard of thrombosis?' He pointed to a dark gobbet on the cut-open heart. 'That's a thrombosis, in the right atrium. Also the heart's enlarged, 630 grammes, a good third bigger than you'd expect for a man of this size. He had a condition that made him susceptible to this...'

I thought, 'We are just meat,' then called it back. Flesh, bodily substance, colons and livers and hearts, had taken on a new wonder. If you had to build a pump, or a gas-exchange system, or a device for absorbing nutrients, you would never dream of using meat.

'And his wife asked for a post-mortem. She wanted to know the cause of death. Although he'd been ill a long time, his death was very sudden. She had looked after him. She wants to know if there was anything else she could have done...'

The cold organs laid on the cold tray. They didn't call out, didn't suggest any great meanings, they were plain and soft and vulnerable, with their billowing smell of meat. After this one last favour, granting absolution to the man's wife, they'd be returned to the body for cremation or burial, returned to the elements.

We all nodded. Enough.

'Are you hungry?' asked Frank. 'Let's go and get a sandwich. That's the tradition.'

Professor Fleming called it 'the natural evidence of our mortality'. Hearts and lungs, a colon that could be a pig's. That's the deal: if we are to be alive and available for joy and discovery, then it's as an animal body, available for infection and cancer and pain. Not a deal anyone remembers having struck, we just got here, but it's not as though we don't negotiate.

In the staff common room there were low upholstered benches and a water cooler. The windows gave views of car parks and newly built houses beyond. A leaf, swirled up in the breeze, flattened itself against the glass, a gull wheeled in the air. God knows, someone has to plead for the non-human and cry halt to our rapacity, even if he has antibiotics and antiseptics in his rucksack. Or maybe that's the beginning of a truce.

The doctors' conversation soon turned to hospital politics and the dread hand of management. Enough indeed. Enough bodily marvels for one day. I left them to their work just as visiting hour was beginning, and the foyer filled with people. The heart smell haunted me, for a while it was unshakeable, as though, like a wolf, I could sense it everywhere; in the old and middle-aged and babes in arms, all seeking their way towards their relatives and friends. It felt surprisingly good to be part of that rough tribe of the mortal, and good to be well, able to stride outside again, back into the cool March breeze. ■

Sitka Spruce, Cape Blanco State Park, Curry County, Oregon
Photograph by Robert Adams

SECOND NATURE

The de-landscaping of the American West

Jonathan Raban

When I was seventeen in 1959, the lake was as wild a place as I knew. My friend Jeremy Hooker and I would arrive there at around four a.m. in early summer, ditch our bikes in the tangle of rhododendrons, and pick out the narrow path by torchlight as we tiptoed, in existentialist duffel coats, through the brush. Still a long way from the water, we moved like burglars, since we attributed to the carp extraordinary sagacity and guile, along with an extreme aversion to human trespassers on its habitat. Crouched on our knees, speaking in whispers, we assembled our split-cane rods. In the windless dark, the lake's dim ebony sheen was at once sinister and promising. Somewhere out there, deep down, lay Leviathan, or at least his shy but powerful cyprinid cousin.

Our style of fishing was minimalist – no weights, no float, nothing but a hook concealed in a half-crown-sized ball of bread paste, attached to 150 yards or so of nylon monofilament. Though the fish in the lake ran to 20lbs and more, our lines were of 6lbs breaking-strain. The carp, we believed, had eyes so keen that it would baulk at nylon any thicker than gossamer 2X, soaked in strong tea to camouflage it on the muddy bottom. Before first light, and the first *woo-woo-woo-woo*ing of a wood pigeon in the trees, like a breathless child blowing over the neck of a bottle, we'd cast our baited hooks far out, settle our rods between two forked twigs, and squeeze a bead of paste on to the line between the open reel and the first rod ring. A quivering movement of the bead would signal that a carp was showing interest in the bait. The rest was watching, waiting, taking gulps of hot coffee from a shared flask, smoking Anchor cigarettes, and talking in a conspiratorial murmur about books and girls.

The lake slowly paled, with helical twists of mist rising from the water. As the sun showed through the woods, a big carp jumped, crashing back like a paving stone dropped from the sky and leaving behind a pin-sharp, reminiscent after-image of olive and gold. We strained for signs of moving fish – the sudden flap of a disturbed lily pad, or a string of tiny bubbles filtering to the surface – and, tense with expectation, willed the telltale beads to tremble into life.

We nearly always had the lake entirely to ourselves. It was out of bounds to the boys in the prep school, a converted Queen Anne manor, in whose estate it stood, and we regarded it – and the permission we had from the headmaster to fish there – as our exclusive privilege. The lake was no more than two acres at most, but, with its resident water rats, moorhens and wagtails, its visiting herons and kingfishers, and its enormous, mysterious fish, it felt like a sufficient world, magically remote from Lymington, Hants, a few miles to the west.

As often as not, the carp disdained our bait, and we'd leave at mid-morning, five Anchors apiece for the worse, but on good days, usually after hours of waiting, the bead of paste would twitch, then stop, then twitch again. This could go on for half an hour or more. The carp – with its big, lippy, toothless mouth – is a leisurely feeder: it rootles along the bottom, vacuuming up silt; swills it about in search of delicacies, then ejects the muddy mouthful like a wine taster using a spittoon. The bead would rise an inch or two towards the first ring, and sink slowly back. Then, either nothing at all would happen, or, at last, the line might begin to slide steadily through the rings, uncoiling from the open face of the fixed-spool reel. That was the moment to strike – to lift the rod, engage the pick-up on the reel and find oneself attached to what felt like a speeding locomotive as the carp ran for the deep, the rod bent in a U, the taut line razoring through the water. Of the fish we hooked, most were quickly lost when they jumped, doubled back or buried themselves among the lilies, but sometimes we'd have a thrilling twenty-minute battle, never seeing the carp until the last moments, when it flopped, exhausted, over the rim of the extended landing net. Out of its element, it looked prehistoric, like a paunchy coelacanth; its armour of interlocking golden scales glistering in the sunshine, its great mouth framing an O of astonishment and indignity at its capture. Still jittery from our encounter with this creature from a netherworld, we'd unhook it, weigh it and return it to the water.

Jerry later wrote a fine poem about these expeditions, titled 'Tench Fisher's Dawn' (there were tench in the lake, too, though they evidently interested him more than they did me), whose last line reads, 'Then, casting out, we're suddenly in touch.' In touch with what, though? *Nature* was how it felt at the time, an engagement with the wild. But in England, nature and culture are so intimately entwined that their categorical separation is a false distinction. At the lake at Walhampton, the two were fused. The rhododendron jungle where we hid our bikes was made up of species introduced to England from the Alps, North America and the Himalayas between the seventeenth and nineteenth centuries. Carp were first imported from Eastern Europe in the early thirteenth century. Until the monastery's dissolution in 1539, Walhampton was one of the many outposts of the powerful Augustinian priory of Christchurch, Twineham. The lake was certainly artificial – probably a later enlargement of a monastic fish pond – and our fat carp were the direct descendants of the exotics farmed by the monks, or so I like to think now. The surrounding woods were sculpted by 'improvers' in the late eighteenth or early nineteenth century. We were fishing in the deep waters of several hundred years of patient engineering, cultivation, fish husbandry and landscape gardening – not first but second nature.

As the word itself says, landscape is land-shaped, and all England is landscape – a country whose deforestation began with Stone Age agriculturalists, and whose last old-growth trees were consumed by the energy industry of the time, the sixteenth-century charcoal-burners; where the Norfolk Broads – now in danger of becoming an inlet of the North Sea – are the flooded open-cast mines of medieval peat diggers; where the chief nesting places of its birds are hedges, many of which go back to hawthorn plantings by the Saxons; where domesticated sheep have cleanly shaven every hill; where coverts, coppices and spinneys exist (or existed until the ban) as subsidized amenities for the fox-hunting brigade; where barely a patch of earth can be found that hasn't been adapted to a specific human use.

The English have a genius for incorporating industrial and technological change into their versions of both nature and the picturesque. It's hard now to imagine the wholesale wreckage of the countryside by huge gangs of Irish navigators, otherwise known as 'navvies', as they dug and tunnelled their way through England during the canal-mania period of the Industrial Revolution. But spool on another century and a bit, and the canals – still busy with commercial barge traffic – had become symbols of all that was green, pleasant and tranquil in the land.

When my father was abroad in North Africa, Italy and Palestine during the Second World War, my mother kept him supplied with a series of slender books, printed on thin, grainy war-issue paper and illustrated with evocative wood engravings, about British churches and cathedrals, pubs, cottages, ancient market towns, gardens and scenic byways, designed to remind the patriotic serviceman of the world he was fighting for. One book in the series, brought home to Norfolk by my father in 1945, and a particular favourite of mine, was devoted to the canals of England and their locks and bridges, now solidly established as key items in the paraphernalia of conventional English pastoral.

Many city children of my generation got their first experience of nature courtesy of the Luftwaffe, when bombed-out houses were transformed into little wildernesses of thistle, teasel, willowherb and loosestrife. Redstarts and other birds nested in crannies in the ruins, among staircases leading to nowhere, peeling wallpaper and upper-storey fireplaces, still with ashes in the grate, now open to the sky. The bomb sites, where I yearned in vain to be allowed to play, appeared to me to be immemorial landscape features, full of character and mystery, and one of the major attractions of family visits to London, Liverpool and Birkenhead in the late 1940s and early 1950s.

Or one might look at Turner's astonishing *Rain, Steam and Speed – The Great Western Railway* (exhibited 1844), whose rendering of elemental swirl and tumult makes it close kin to his *Snow Storm – Steam-Boat off a Harbour's Mouth...* (1842). But where the earlier painting shows the paddle wheeler all but overwhelmed by a hurricane-strength wind and terrifyingly steep cross-seas, the train in *Rain, Steam and Speed* is not the victim of the wild weather but its apparent prime mover. To the peaceful, lately sunlit arcadia of Maidenhead, with its plough, scarified hare and the unruffled Thames below, where two figures are seated in a punt (gudgeon fishing, I suspect), has come this roaring Boanerges, son of thunder, raising a perfect storm. On the final page of his *J.M.W. Turner: 'A Wonderful Range of Mind'*, John Gage asks, 'Has the railway desecrated the beautiful stretch of the Thames it crosses here at Maidenhead?' But it's surely clear from the painting that Turner loves the locomotive, with the blazing inferno of its firebox eerily exposed. He paints the newfangled intruder on the landscape as a force of nature in its own right. Gage remarks on the 'light-heartedness' of the picture's imagery; its wittiest touch is that the gudgeon fishers, if that's what they are, don't even bother to look up in wonder at the transcendent marvel of their age. But then they're English, born to a casual phlegmatic acceptance of astounding alterations to the landscape, and perhaps the train and Brunel's great flat-arched viaduct have already been absorbed into their sense of the natural order of things. If you're bred to living in second nature, it's relatively easy to find room in it for a Firefly-class steam engine alongside the gudgeon and the plough.

When I moved to the Pacific Northwest in 1990, I felt at a loss. Accustomed to living in England's secondary nature, I had difficulty reading a landscape in which so much primary nature showed through the patchy overlay of around 140 years of white settlement and enterprise. Hunting for a workable analogy, I tried to see myself as a visitor to Roman Britain at the end of the second century, taking in the new cities, the network of paved highways, the agricultural estates and military installations, superimposed on a land lightly occupied by tribal people. But that conceit was flawed: the British tribes had permanently altered the land with mines, farms, forts, and ritual and funerary monuments long before the Romans came, while the Northwest Indians left few visible traces of their 12,000-year habitation. West of the Cascade Range, where wood rots fast in the soggy climate, the Indian past faded continually behind the ongoing present, like the dissolving wake of a cedar canoe. Artefacts like painted chests, ritual masks and wall hangings survived, but whole towns were reclaimed by the forest within a generation, leaving little more than overgrown shell middens to mark where they'd stood. Wherever the land was significantly shaped, or 'scaped', the work appeared to have been done just recently – a spreading accumulation of raw concrete, pressed steel, brick, sheetrock, telephone poles, pavement, fencing, neon, glass and vinyl, scattered in piecemeal fashion across a nature whose essential bone structure of mountains, lakes, forest and sea inlets was still so prominent that the most ambitious attempts to build on and subdue it looked tentative and provisional.

Living in Seattle, one would have to entomb oneself in the basement to avoid the view. On clear days, the snowy bulk of Mount Rainier, high as the Matterhorn, towers over the city, which squats on the edge of Puget Sound, more than a hundred fathoms deep. The lower slopes of the Cascades to the east and the Olympics to the west are thickly furred with forest, or the appearance of forest (for most of the visible timber is actually second- or third-growth 'tree farms'). Black bears and cougars forage in the suburbs; threatened Chinook salmon flounder through the shipping on the Duwamish Waterway, struggling upstream to spawn and die; from my window, less than two miles north of downtown, I watch bald eagles on their regular east–west flight path over the Lake Washington Ship Canal; a walker in this city can see killer whales breaching, California sea lions hauled out on docks, beavers, coyotes, opossums, foxes, raccoons.

Nearly four million people live in the coastal sprawl of metropolitan Seattle, and there can be very few cities of its size where it's so easy to feel like a trespasser on the habitat of other creatures, and to be uneasily aware that those creatures, given half a chance, would quickly regain possession of their old freehold. Squint, and you can imagine the wood-frame houses collapsing into greenery, and large mammals denning in abandoned malls. It's hardly surprising that the urban Pacific Northwest is home to a strain of radical environmentalism whose aim is not just to conserve what's still left of nature in these parts, but to dismantle the machinery of industrial civilization and restore large tracts of country to the wild.

Whenever a bridge on a forest road washes out in a winter storm, a lobby springs up to demand that the entire road be condemned. Some dams are being breached to return rivers to the salmon, and many more are targeted for demolition. The movement, supported by a string of court victories, to prohibit – or drastically restrict – logging, mining and livestock grazing on public lands has steadily gained momentum over the last decade, even though the Bush administration and – until January 2007 – the Republican-controlled Congress, have fought to unstitch the environmental legislation of the Clinton years. Gray wolves, fishers, wolverines and grizzly bears – all species that survive here in minuscule numbers at present – are being reintroduced. (In the case of the widely feared grizzlies, Canadians are making the reintroductions in British Columbia and the undocumented bears are immigrating into Washington state.) At present, two bills making their way through Congress will soon add 200 square miles of mountain lakes, old-growth forest and river valleys to existing 'wilderness areas' within an hour's drive from Seattle. As the Wilderness Act of 1964 put it: 'A wilderness, in contrast with those areas where man and his own works dominate the landscape, is hereby recognized as an area where the earth and its community of life are untrammelled by man, where man himself is a visitor who does not remain.'

This is landscaping in reverse. Its main advocates are politicians, activists and non-profit foundations in large coastal cities such as Seattle and Portland, Oregon, who argue that the rise in 'quality of life assets', created by such wilding of the countryside, can amply compensate for the loss of jobs in traditional rural industries such as logging, mining, ranching and farming. 'Nature' and 'Solitude' – those Emersonian essay titles – have a potentially higher cash value, say the conservationists, than horizontal trees or pockets of natural gas trapped in the coal seams underlying a beautiful mountain pass. When land is designated as wilderness, property prices immediately increase in its vicinity, and so does the flow of cash brought into the area by campers, hikers, hunters, fly-fishermen, snowshoers and mountaineers.

For the economist in a city office, it's a simple transfer of figures from column to column, from Agriculture & Industry to Services & Retail Trade: if the loss in one is equalled or exceeded by the gain in the other, nobody should have cause for complaint, at least in the long run. But that's not how it's seen in the country, where the fast-advancing cause of wilderness has been met with very modified rapture.

To the loggers and farmers, man-the-visitor-who-does-not-remain is just another tourist; a member of a breed much disliked in the rural West for its presumed wealth, ignorance and disdain for the concerns of people who work the land instead of using it as a weekend playground. Hundred-year-old lumber and market communities, faced with the prospect of a radical shift in their economies, can see the future all too clearly in the shape of the 'gateway towns' that rim national parks like Yellowstone, Glacier and Yosemite; those desolate strips of competing motels, minimarts, gas stations, gift shops and fast-food outlets. Whatever these places may once have been, their only business now is to make the beds, pump the gas, serve the meals and wash the dirty linen of the tourists – occupations in which there's money but little dignity.

And it's the assault on their dignity that so offends the country-dwellers: the treatment of the logger, proud of his skilled and dangerous job, as a reckless vandal; the subordination of rural work to the recreational interests of urban sportsmen and nature lovers; the assumption of intellectual superiority by city-based environmentalists, with their mantra of 'best available science', routinely abbreviated to BAS. The West is in the middle of a furious conflict between the city and the country, in part a class war, in part a generational one, which has significant political consequences.

In the 2004 general election, every city in the United States with more than 500,000 inhabitants returned a majority vote for John Kerry. The election was won for Bush and the Republicans in the outer suburbs and the rural hinterlands. Much was made of 'red states' and 'blue states', but the great rift was between the blue cities and the red countryside. Environmental politics, in the form of fervent local quarrels over land use, were at the heart of this division. Beneath the talk of Iraq, health care, terrorism, gun control, abortion and all the rest lay a barely articulated but passionate dispute about the nature of nature in America.

Forty miles east of Seattle, the crest of the Cascade Range, punctuated along its length by snow-mantled volcanoes, runs north to south, dividing Washington state into two regions. Crossing from one to the other over a mountain pass, you experience in minutes a violent change of climate and culture, as the inky green of Douglas firs, mosses, ferns and salal suddenly gives way to shale, sagebrush, juniper and piñon pine. Annual rainfall plummets from around eighty inches a year to ten or less; incomes and house prices drop; on the car radio, the news on National Public Radio fades into a drizzle of static, its place quickly occupied by a gospel or Spanish-language station. In the newly moistureless atmosphere, the light turns hard and clear, collapsing distances, so that the entire Columbia Basin, an area larger than France, seems to make itself visible all at once: a web of branching canyons, intricate as a leaf skeleton, threaded between bare whaleback hills.

On old maps, it shows as part of the 'Great American Desert' – an arid, treeless expanse, home to jackrabbits and rattlesnakes, fit for human use only for its mineral deposits and as an open range for sheep and cattle grazing on the sage and bunch grass. But the Columbia River and its tributaries, laden with snowmelt from the Cascades and the Rockies, flowed through the canyons, and the pillowy basalt uplands – solidified streams of the molten lava that coursed from the mountains during their formation – were coated in fine wind-blown silt, or loess; soil in which almost anything would grow if it could be moistened with water from the rivers. What would turn into one of the most grandiose landscaping projects on earth began in a modest, ad hoc way, as nineteenth-century white settlers built diversion dams and sluices, and dug canals and ditches, tapping the nearest river for irrigation by using the same minimal technology with which Mesopotamians watered the Iraqi desert from the Euphrates, and the Hohokam Indians of Arizona periodically flooded their parched flatlands on the Gila and Salt rivers 1,500 years ago.

In the national mythology, it's the quintessential American experience to arrive in a wild and inhospitable place, bend raw nature to one's own advantage and make it home. So the land encountered by the Columbia Basin settlers was an American classic: mile upon mile of twiggy sage, spread over bald and shadeless hills, broken by sheer cliffs of fissured rock.

Near the junctions with the Columbia of steep, fast-flowing streams, settlers built weirs to channel water into irrigation ditches that hugged the contour lines and eventually, after a serpentine journey around the countryside, discharged into the main river, several hundred feet below the level of each weir. These 'highline' canals, most of them financed by railroad companies and consortia of city businessmen, opened broad swathes of land for cultivation. Sagebrush was ploughed into fields, fifty-dollar windmills were installed to pump the water to the soil and the lower canyons were transformed into a quilt of farms and orchards.

From the beginning, the US government watched over such private-enterprise schemes like a jealous parent. In the federal imagination, the watering of the dry West presented a fantastic opportunity, at once ideological and practical. The region was still best known for its mining camps, its migrant cattle and migrant men, and for wide-open towns whose success was measured by the number of their saloons, brothels, casinos and murders. Irrigation, on a scale far beyond the means of the private sector, would turn this barely governable land into a settled agrarian democracy – a society of family farmers with family values, beholden to the government for their good fortune. When the National Reclamation Act was passed in 1902, President Theodore Roosevelt called it 'one of the greatest steps not only in the forward progress of the States, but in that of all mankind' and forecast that 'communities flourishing in what is now the desert finally will take their places among the strongest pillars of our Commonwealth'. Reclamation of the soil would bring about a greater reclamation – of morals, manners and citizenship.

The Act's sponsor, a Nevada congressman named Francis Newlands, envisioned that 60 million acres of arid wilderness would eventually come under the plough. The enormous cost of irrigation would be paid for by the sale of public lands to homesteaders on ten-year mortgages. To stop the corporations – especially the railroad companies – from making a government-subsidized land grab, each family would be limited to a maximum of 160 acres and would have to prove permanent residence on their farm.

The plan had the charm of a perpetual motion machine: it would produce a continuously revolving fund of money from a limitless supply of at present useless land, and generate a steadily expanding tax-base of prosperous small farms. It would tame the lawless West, ease overcrowding in the eastern cities, feed the hungry and enrich the nation – all at no cost to the taxpayer. It was the quintessential politicians' dream.

The new US Bureau of Reclamation sent out teams of geologists to scour the West for possible sites for dams, and involved itself in a multitude of schemes, most of which ran awry as irrigation works fell behind schedule, costs overran, and farmers went broke trying to meet their monthly payments on the proceeds of scanty harvests. In 1923, the Secretary of the Interior admitted that, 'Reclamation of arid lands by irrigation from Government funds…is failing on a majority of projects.' Although successive presidents, including Hoover and Coolidge, talked up the federal dream of landscaping the West, it wasn't until the Great Depression and Franklin Roosevelt's New Deal administration, more than thirty years after the passage of the Newlands Act, that the big dams, so long promised, at last began to take real shape.

In 1933, the first concrete was poured at the Boulder Dam across the Colorado River on the Arizona–Nevada border and work started on the Fort Peck Dam across the Missouri in Montana, and the Bonneville and Grand Coulee dams on the Columbia. 'We are in the process of making the American people "dam-minded",' Franklin Roosevelt said at the Grand Coulee site in 1934, where the sheer gigantism of the project made the dam a symbol of national regeneration in hard times. 'The largest structure ever undertaken by man,' Roosevelt called it, and a *New York Times* reporter, travelling with the presidential entourage, tried to convey to his readers the immensity of the Grand Coulee, first in familiar New York terms – 'a structure that will be higher than a forty-storey building, longer than four ocean liners the size of the *Queen Mary*, and almost two city blocks in thickness' – then in terms of the extraterrestrial: 'It stretches across the Columbia like the crenellated wall of a giant fortress built to withstand the artillery of some super-warriors from Mars.'

It took eight years to build, the urgency of its completion mounting every year as conditions in the dust bowl worsened and more than 100,000 homeless farm workers and their families streamed into Washington state. Some found work as labourers on the dams, others as seasonal fruit pickers in the orchards around Wenatchee and Yakima; they set up home in smoky encampments along the Columbia Valley, living in tents, plywood shanties and cardboard boxes. More bold promises were made: irrigation would create farms of ten to forty acres, where half a million refugees from the agricultural catastrophes to the east could be resettled and their self-respect restored.

In 1941, when the dam was finished and the first hydroelectric turbines spinning, the Bonneville Power Administration, a federal agency, hired Woody Guthrie to sing its praises, giving him a month-long contract, a chauffeur-driven Hudson and a $266.66 pay cheque. The short, sparrow-weight folk singer was known to the FBI as Woodrow Wilson Guthrie, a Communist Party sympathizer, whose guitar soundboard carried the message, in big letters, THIS MACHINE KILLS FASCISTS. For four weeks, Guthrie was driven up and down the Columbia between the Bonneville and Grand Coulee dams, during which time he was reported by his driver to have never changed his clothes or taken a bath: 'Poor guy had BO so bad you could hardly stand it.'

If his songs are to be believed, Guthrie's usually sardonic take on the world melted in the face of the Columbia Basin project. 'This is just as close to heaven as my travelling feet have been,' he sung in 'Roll, Columbia, Roll', and seems to have persuaded himself that something not far short of a socialist utopia was dawning in the Pacific Northwest. In a homely voice, pitched midway between a croak and a yodel, he extolled, in 'Pastures of Plenty', the electrification of rural America – lighting farmhouses, powering factories and mills, and the greening of the desert.

Guthrie wrote: 'I saw the Columbia River and the big Grand Coulee Dam from just about every cliff, mountain, tree and post from which it can be seen' – vantage points from which that other panorama, of penniless rural nomads in their Hoovervilles, unfolded all around him. Many of the songs, including 'Talking Dust Bowl (Washington Talking Blues)', are phrased from the point of view of the 'Okie' travelling man, wistfully imagining a settled future on a watered plot, his crops sprouting all around him.

But these songs were thick with cautiously subjunctive 'woulds' and 'coulds' because the irrigation scheme – Grand Coulee's original main purpose – had already been shelved. More than a year before Pearl Harbor, the US government decided that, in view of the 'national defence emergency' created by the war in Europe, only the hydroelectric function of the dam could be justified for the time being, and the green pastures of plenty would have to be put on hold until the end of the war.

Hidden in a cleft between hills of unreclaimed sagebrush, its presence signalled only by converging lines of skyscraper-high transmission towers, the Grand Coulee Dam still has the power to astonish. The front of the dam – where Guthrie admired 'the misty crystal glitter of that wild and windward spray' – is dry now, a stained and weathered concrete cliff, over which the engineers release water from Lake Roosevelt above the dam only for son et lumière shows, put on for tourists on summer nights. Wedged snugly into the landscape, the Grand Coulee has become a period piece, like the Mussolini-era railway stations that are its close contemporaries.

Though many other dams have since been built across the river – between the Bonneville Dam, upstream of Portland, Oregon, and the Grand Coulee, there are now eleven dams in US territory, plus a further three in Canada – the Grand Coulee is still the Columbia

Basin's haunting genius loci, the prime shaper of its landscape, and the hulking embodiment of the idea that man's mastery over nature had reached such a degree that he could work transformative miracles of the kind traditionally performed by gods: water into megawatts, desert into garden, wilderness into civilization.

It wasn't until 1950, under the presidency of Harry Truman, that the great federal irrigation scheme at last got under way. Nearly sixty years on, Truman, Guthrie, both Roosevelts and a string of presidents in between, would be astonished by the appearance of the rural wonderland they conjured into being in songs and speeches. On a recent drive across the Columbia Plateau, I had Guthrie singing on the CD player as I took in mile after bullet-straight mile of country whose desolate character remains obstinately unsoftened by no end of technological ingenuity and agricultural enterprise.

The roads run north to south and east to west, one mile apart in each direction. Aside from the occasional line of irrigated poplars, planted as shelter belts, the only verticals in the landscape are telephone poles; otherwise it's like a gigantic sheet of graph paper. For this one must thank Thomas Jefferson who, in the 1780s, inaugurated the marvellous eighteenth-century rationalistic scheme of taming unruly American nature by imposing on it the 'township and range' system.

From an arbitrary point on the Ohio River, where it crosses the western boundary of Pennsylvania, surveyors were to map their way across the rapidly expanding territory of the United States, dividing it into 'townships', each measuring six miles by six, and further subdivided into thirty-six 'sections' of one square mile apiece. Section 16, near the centre of the notional township, three squares down from its northern limit and three from its western one, was to be set aside for the purposes of public education. In effect, Jefferson flung out a potentially infinite graticule across thousands of miles of as-yet-undiscovered country, planting phantom towns, each with its schoolhouse or college on every Section 16, wherever it might fall – on the craggy top of a mountain, or the muddy bottom of a lake.

Although actual townships never conformed to Jefferson's grand plan but grew up for the usual reasons – because they were on a river, a cattle trail, a railroad, or, later, an interstate highway – the survey method, with its six-mile squares and square-mile sections, has improbably continued into the present. Wherever you are, in wide-open prairie or deep forest, you stand in a numbered section of a numbered township. Roads hew to the lines of the speculative graticule, paying no attention to contours, which makes driving in the West feel like being on watch aboard a ship on automatic pilot, locked to a rigid compass course. I was going south, on a road named 'QNW'. Longitudinal roads were designated by letters, latitudinal ones by numbers: if one could count and spell, it was impossible to get lost on this dusty tableland, now more geometry than nature.

Each field occupies a full section – a 640-acre square, watered by a half-mile-long centre-pivot sprinkler, making a perfect circle of green or chocolate-brown in the pale-olive desert. The computer-controlled sprinklers, driven by electric motors, trundle slowly round and round on wheeled undercarriages, taking a day or more to complete a single circuit. The fields' edges are strewn with the handiwork of the water engineers: pipes and spigots, squat pumphouses, lateral ditches and canals that, even after all these years, still look like rawly excavated trenches in the earth.

Miles of this flat, robotic agriculture separate farmhouse from farmhouse – a far cry from what was envisioned in 1952, when a lottery was opened to Second World War veterans, who had first dibs on eighty-acre parcels of irrigated land, each just one-eighth of a section, for an initial investment of $4,600. The federal planners were incorrigible sentimentalists, still clinging, in the mid-twentieth century, to that peculiarly American mythologization of the small farmer as the fount of human goodness and the small farm as the essential building block in the atomic structure of democracy. 'Farmers are the chosen people of God, if ever he had a chosen people, whose breasts he has made his peculiar deposit for substantial and genuine virtue,' wrote Jefferson. The planners saw the Columbia Plateau as an organic society of pocket-sized family farms, like an epic Robert Frost poem, full of salt-of-the-earth types mending walls and fences, planting seeds, their long two-pointed ladders aimed at heaven through the trees.

What actually emerged was an enormous tract of government-subsidized agribusiness, a monotonous and lonely landscape dedicated to the mass production of such valuable items as the fast-food frozen French fry. Within the federally regulated area of the plateau, the family farms quickly swelled to a dozen times their original size, while on its fringes the agricultural corporations moved in during the 1970s and 1980s, to piggyback on the federal project, using cheap federal electricity to pump cheap federal water over farms whose acreages are measured in the tens of thousands. One barely credible statistic: in 2001, the *New York Times* reported that Columbia Basin farmers were paying $1.50 per megawatt of electricity at a time when a megawatt was commanding a price of $375 to $400 on the open market.

Sharing the narrow roads with eighteen-wheeler refrigerated trucks, catching intermittent glimpses of the Columbia River, flanked by sheer cliffs of dark basalt, nearly 1,000 feet below the plateau, I thought of how I'd been brought up with the quaint idea that cultivation gives a human shape and scale to the land. But this land seemed now less friendly to the human than when the farmers first arrived. The rectilinear severity of its roads and its vast identical fields of beet and potatoes robbed it of distance and perspective. Its chief architectural feature wasn't the farmhouse but the 'facility' – the white metal shed, spread over the best part of an acre, where the vegetables were processed and packaged in the loading bays full of eighteen-wheelers, lined up hull to hull. From these grim facilities came French fries – machine-cut, parboiled, pre-fried, flash-frozen – along with tinfoil sachets of instant mashed potato and the rubbery, vermicular tangles that pass for hash browns on the breakfast plates of every chain restaurant at every freeway exit in America.

I stopped for lunch at Mattawa, a familiar-looking grid of bungalows and trailer homes, just big enough to support a supermarket and high school. SERVICIOS EN ESPANOL said the signboard by the Mormon tabernacle, an unnecessary piece of information since everything in Mattawa was so obviously *en Español* – the Catholic church; the grocery-cum-video store; the hair salon; the laundromat; the family clinic; the rival *taquerias*, La Popular and El Jato, where a Mexican soap opera was turned up to full volume on the TV.

Mattawa was a displaced *barrio*, more than 1,000 miles from home, with the melancholy air that displacement brings. Its per capita income, as I later found out, is around $7,500 per year; a minimum-wage town, and typical of the Spanish-speaking settlements scattered over the plateau. Where the town peters out near the Shell gas station, the facilities begin: one is a potato-packing plant, one makes malt from barley, a third produces compressed hay cubes for cattle feed. They are all owned and managed by Anglos, with Mexican, Guatemalan or Mexican-American workforces. During the picking season – from May to September – the Hispanic population doubles, as truckloads of migrant labourers pour into the Columbia Basin, filling spare rooms and run-down cheap motels, with many living in encampments hardly distinguishable from the Hoovervilles of the Great Depression.

From the Mattawa restaurant, sucking on a bottle of Pacifico beer, waiting for tamales to arrive, it was hard to conceive that such gigantic investment – of rhetoric, sentiment, rural nostalgia, as well as now incalculable billions of public money – could have resulted in a farmscape so characterless and bleak, the majority of whose inhabitants appeared little better off than the dust-bowl refugees for whom this land had been designed as an agrarian sanctuary.

The map made me stop at Desert Aire, six miles south of Mattawa. It lay right on the river's edge – a powerful lure – but what interested me most was its street plan. According to the map, it was a maze of culs-de-sac and crescents, with hardly a straight line in sight, in defiance of the universal reverence for the austere grid. It boasted an airstrip with a limp windsock and a narrow, looping golf course that functioned as the town's main street. The buildings were mostly 'manufactured homes', ready-made houses in an assortment of styles – ranch, Queen Anne, New England colonial – that had been trucked out to the site and craned into place. Started by a developer in 1970, Desert Aire looked as if it had failed so far to take root; its curvy streets empty of people, its front yards neat but bare, a social experiment in a waste of sagebrush that was still in its beta-testing stage.

I drove down to the river – or to what had once been the river. A line of immature poplars shadowed a beach of thin shale. A rectangle, the size of a modest building plot, had been roughly excavated to create what the sign above it said was a marina, which held a single short pontoon but no boats. The beach fronted a mile-and-a-half-wide stretch of inert, tea-coloured water, formerly the Columbia. A couple of miles to the south lay the pale concrete ramparts of the Priest Rapids Dam.

Before the dams, the Columbia was one of the great rivers of the world. Black-and-white photographs (handily collected in William D. Layman's *River of Memory: The Everlasting Columbia*) show it in its glory – its tumbling falls, narrow chutes, white-water rapids, whirlpools, slow, reflective deeps, changing continuously in character from mile to mile. On one page, it's a level drift through a fringing forest of willows, cottonwoods and alders, its surface lightly patterned by arabesques of current; on the next, it's a torrent of boiling milk.

As each dam went up, the river rose behind it, drowning its natural banks. Sandbars, islands, trees and farms went under. Where it had once thundered, it suddenly fell silent. People euphemistically renamed the dead water between the dams as 'lakes'; at Desert Aire, I was standing on the beach of Priest Rapids Lake. But it wasn't a lake; the best that could be said for it was that it was like an urban reservoir, a holding tank to supply water for irrigation and energy to drive the turbines inside the dams. From each dam, lines of pylons marched every which way over the bare hills, like gangs of thieves making off with their swag, robbing the Columbia of its life in order to sell corporate farmers electricity at the laughable price of $1.50 a megawatt.

For conservationists, the salmon is the paramount symbol of life in the river and the courts are full of ongoing litigation brought on the salmon's behalf – especially the case for demolishing the dams on the Snake River, the Columbia's biggest tributary. But as a sometime carp fisherman, I have another fish in mind – a creature bigger, stranger and more deserving of wonder than the salmon, which has the conformist mentality of a drudge on a commuter train, as it travels en masse between fresh water and the ocean. My candidate is the Columbia white sturgeon.

Somewhere down at the bottom of Priest Rapids Lake, grubbing its way in near darkness through the sludge, there must be a surviving sturgeon or two – a fish that might have sprung from the imagination of a myth-maker, its size and power commensurate with those of the Columbia River itself before humans destroyed its upper reaches. The sturgeon can grow to twenty feet long, live for more than a hundred years, and weigh up to 1,800 lbs. It has small myopic eyes, the streamlined build of a pike or a U-boat, with a tapering snout from which trail four whiskery barbules, and hose-like lips which it extends, concertina-style, to savour likely morsels. Its only true bones are in its head; its body is a mass of cartilage and muscle, armoured with rows of interlocking, diamond-shaped, razor-edged plates. It's an opportunistic eater, foraging on plants, live and dead salmon, shrimp, lampreys, shellfish; one sturgeon, caught on the Snake, was found to have scoffed a bushel of onions, and pictures of trophy sturgeon, taken before strict size limits came into force, make their grinning captors look as if they should have been the fish' lunch.

Before the dams, sturgeon were anadromous, swimming freely between the river and the sea, spawning many times during their long lives, unlike Pacific salmon, which spawn once and die. Below the

The Grand Coulee Dam, partially completed, June 15, 1941

Bonneville Dam, where there's a healthy sturgeon fishery, that's still true; but above it, the fish are trapped, too big to negotiate the ladders used by the ever-decreasing runs of salmon, and their numbers are shrinking fast. There are monster sturgeon that were striplings in their thirties when the Bonneville and Grand Coulee dams were built. Trying to recreate whatever dim, ichthyotic memory they may have of fast-running water, they hang around the spillways of the dams at spawning time and lay eggs in the shallows there, some of which actually hatch into fry. But these landlocked sturgeon, trying as best they can to adapt to their changed circumstances, are slowly losing the fight against extinction.

At Desert Aire, I spent a half-hour studying the water through Polaroid dark glasses like a fisherman, methodically searching each quadrant for rising strings of telltale bubbles, dark submarine shadows, distant humps or swirls. But no fish – sturgeon or otherwise – stirred. The water appeared lifeless except for occasional patches where it was frosted by a temporary and feeble breeze. It's said that sturgeon, like carp, sometimes spontaneously fling themselves skyward. Suppose, on a still night, a spry, eighteen-foot nonagenarian were to leap for the stars: the ensuing crash would scare Desert Aire's entire population out of their beds. That would be something to see.

A little way beyond the Priest Rapids Dam, I crossed the Columbia on a road trending south-west, which led through the most undisturbed 'brush-steppe' habitat in America, where no range cattle intrude on the sagebrush dotted with wild phlox, evening primroses and Piper's daisies, the unchallenged territory of mountain elk, mule deer, bobcats, coyotes and porcupines. Peregrine and prairie falcons ride on thermals overhead. For thirty miles, one sees the land as it was on the Columbia Plateau to the east, before ranchers – then irrigators and factory farmers – changed its face for the worse. Even the road – State Route 240 – has natural bends in it, to conform with the swell of the hills.

'Fat Man' did this. The plutonium that powered the bomb that was detonated over Nagasaki, immediately killing 40,000, was manufactured at the Hanford Engineer Works. The Manhattan Project required a site remote from human habitation, with access to unlimited supplies of water and electricity. Everything necessary was here, where the Columbia made a crooked dog's-leg swing to the east, then north, then south, to frame a level stretch of country the size of Hertfordshire. The riverbank farmers were evicted and the place was code-named Site W.

From the road, there wasn't much to see beyond the prohibitive barbed-wire fencing: the cluster of white buildings, six or seven miles off, looked like an innocuous farm town; they might have been grain silos, barns, a water tower, a church. More buildings tapered in the haze to the east, but nothing in view helped one to imagine the real scale of the plant, which, by the summer of 1944, employed several thousand more people than Fat Man killed, and which went on to make its specialized contribution to the US nuclear arsenal for another forty years.

Hanford is routinely described as the most polluted nuclear site in the nation. Some 53 million gallons of highly radioactive waste are stored in underground tanks, all of them obsolete, many of them leaking, and clean-up workers keep on finding unexpected burial grounds for irradiated reactor fuel along the west bank of the river. The business of decontaminating this lethal dump began in 1989, shortly after it stopped producing weapons-grade plutonium. Every year, the estimated costs rise, and the deadline for completion – when the waste will be vitrified into glass and safely removed – is projected further into the future. At present, that date is 2048; in a year or two, no doubt, a further decade will be added to it.

Yet the secrecy and danger of the site kept irrigation, farming and hydroelectric schemes away from the river and made a nature reserve of the land, which in 2000 became, by presidential proclamation, the Hanford Reach National Monument. So the A-bomb restored more than 600 square miles of what used once to be orchards and farms to at least the appearance of the wild, and left the Columbia to flow relatively freely between the Priest Rapids Dam and the McNary Dam, fifty-one miles downstream. But it's a spooky kind of wild, where the razor-wire security fence and the black-trefoil-on-yellow-ground danger sign are part of the furniture, and the jackrabbits are lightly irradiated with trace amounts of radioactive iodine-129.

I drove on to Richland, at the junction of the Yakima River and the Columbia, once a small farm town, then a dormitory for workers on the Manhattan Project, and now, attached to its close neighbours – Pasco and Kennewick – part of a charmless urban agglomeration known as the Tri Cities. This is a sixteen-mile sprawl of malls, parking lots and high-rise offices, through which the two rivers flow as mere impediments to their more perfect union. At my first attempt to find the centre of Richland, I overshot, and found myself on the wrong side of the Columbia, in Pasco. On my second, I landed up in Kennewick. On my third, I clung to the west bank of the Columbia and found a hotel room that overlooked the river. My ambition was to see it move.

But an evening wind had sprung up and the ruffled tan water looked no less reservoir-like than it had done at Desert Aire. There's a drop of seventy-five feet along the Hanford Reach – not much over a length of fifty miles, but enough to impart life and motion, and make it by far the best salmon-spawning ground on the dammed section of the river. Disappointed, I took myself off on a tour of Richland, looking for somewhere to eat that was neither a Red Robin, McDonald's, Pizza Hut, Arby's or Jack in the Box, nor a chain restaurant catering to conventioneers, and came across the local high school. What was one to make of a city whose high-school sports teams call themselves the Richland Bombers, and proudly wear a logo consisting of a capital R superimposed on a pluming mushroom cloud? After a long search, I found a small bistro tucked inside an unpromising-looking office complex, where, over the best bowl of Ukrainian borscht I've ever tasted, I wondered if Richland had many visitors from Nagasaki.

Shortly after dawn the next morning, I went down to the river to take another look. The air was perfectly still, and thin spirals of mist were rising from the glassy surface, just as they used to do at Walhampton. Inshore, the water was dead, but close to midstream, 150 yards out, the current showed in a scribble of lines and curlicues, bright silver in the early sun. Some way upstream, I heard the splash of a jumping fish and saw the concentric ripples it had left behind turn oblong as the river's thrust distorted them. A late-running fall chinook, probably, still trying to rid itself of sea lice. To get to Richland, it would have had to struggle up the ladders of four hydroelectric dams – a killer journey that only a small minority of fish survive. Safe now in Hanford Reach, it would spawn and promptly die. After salmon-spawning time on Pacific Northwest rivers, the stench is terrible, the gravelly shallows full of putrefying corpses, but the smell – strong enough to make one gag – is a measure of the river's health, and in recent years it's grown steadily fainter as more and more salmon runs, including that of the Columbia chinook, are listed under the Endangered Species Act.

Immediately south of the Tri Cities, where the Snake River joins the Columbia, commercial river traffic starts. Grain barges, bound for the container terminal in Portland, Oregon from as far inland as Lewiston in Idaho, pass through the locks that are built into the eight dams on the combined Snake–Columbia navigation. The busy road along the Columbia's east bank was lined with wharves and with facilities belonging to industrial agriculture giants such as J. R. Simplot, ConAgra and AgriNorthwest. As I turned east, into the valley of the Walla Walla River and its dozens of small tributary creeks, marked by winding lines of cottonwoods, farmhouses were suddenly within hailing distance of each other. Fields came in all shapes and sizes. A horse at grass stood in the shade of an old tree. At the foot of the sagebrush hills and canyons lay exactly the countryside – the multicoloured patchwork of family farms – that the apostles of irrigation had designed and legislated for the Columbia Plateau. But what federal laws and money could never achieve was this kind of untidy, impromptu landscape, which had been settled by white farmers since the 1850s, and now might almost be mistaken for a stretch of rural Kent.

The cause for this change of character, and the source of the multitude of creeks, were the cloud-stopping Blue Mountains to the south and east. Low by the standards of the mountainous West, the Blues rose to around 5,000 feet – sufficient to increase the rainfall from six or seven inches a year to ten, eleven, twelve, just over the dividing line that separates 'semi-arid' from 'arid' land. Irrigation is still necessary, but it is of a piece with the landscape, small-scale, improvised. I stopped by one irrigation ditch, so narrow that I could almost have jumped across it, and watched clear water burbling over the lip of a shallow home-made weir. Its grassy banks were still – at the turn of October into November – speckled with wild flowers.

I had an appointment with Rick Small, a winemaker whose vineyard was in the hills to the north of the valley. When I could afford them, I'd much enjoyed his Woodward Canyon Cabernet Sauvignons, boutique wines that start at $40-plus a bottle, and are scored in the 90s by Robert Parker's *Wine Advocate*. I parked the car outside the nineteenth-century farmhouse where Woodward Canyon has its tasting room, and rode with Small up from the green valley into the bare hills to his vineyard.

'My wife hates this bit,' he said, as the truck took a tight corner, and hurtled up a narrow rutted track, roaring in first gear and raising a storm of brown dust behind it. The land was 'rolling', but the word conveys a gentleness entirely absent here. These hills rolled as a gale-torn sea rolls, in lurching peaks and troughs. As we kept on climbing, sage and thistle abruptly gave way to terraces of trellised vines on a slope as steep as the face of a wave. We stopped at the summit, beside three big water tanks, and Small liberated his young German shepherd from the cab.

Below, his forty acres fell away from the south-east to the south-west, tracking the daily path of the sun. The vines, brown now, were decorated with streamers of silver foil to scare the birds. Here and there, a bunch of unpicked grapes remained, their skin wrinkled but their taste still fresh and sweet. Rick Small, lean, bald and buff, dog capering around his heels, led me through the terraces. My local wine merchant in Seattle had told me that Small was an 'enthusiast' – an understatement. 'I was born to do this,' he said. He'd grown up on this land, where his grandfather and his father had been wheat farmers. In 1981, when the Washington state wine industry, now second to California's, was still barely fledged, he planted his first vines.

I said that wine grapes must be the last remaining crop from which a good living in these parts could be made on such a tiny acreage.

'So long as you have vertical integration. If you grow your own grapes, make your own wine, and be your own sales rep, yes, forty acres can make economic sense – all that, plus the passion for it. And patience. It may take twelve, fifteen years to get an idea of whether a grape is planted in the right place.'

On the excavated sides of the terraces, he showed me how unevenly the loess had settled on the basalt underneath. In places, the layer of silt was seven or eight feet deep; elsewhere, just a few inches. I rubbed a pinch of loess between forefinger and thumb; it felt as fine and smoothly lubricant as talc. A crumbled fragment of basalt was riddled with small bubbles – pockets of 10 or 15-million-year-old air, trapped when the immense, successive tides of molten lava rolled over the Columbia Basin, covering it to a depth of up to 16,000 feet.

Small's Merlot grapes liked to be featherbedded in an ample layer of silt, and the tone in which he mentioned this had in it a faint but distinct hint of moral disapproval. What he wanted me to admire was the Spartan fortitude of his Cabernets.

'See? It's practically growing straight from the rock. It's amazing. The silt's so thin there that you'd think nothing would grow. But that's cab. Not much fruit, and they're rooted quite far apart, but look at that determination. It's do or die.'

It was in this spirit that he kept his vines thirsty. We were standing on a latitude exactly midway between that of coastal Bordeaux and inland Burgundy, and I asked him if – given France's generous rainfall – he'd take it as a blessing or a curse.

'I can manage my moisture – that's a great part of being here.'

The well at the bottom of the slope went nearly 800 feet down. The water was then pumped another 300 feet up to the tanks on the summit, from where Small dribbled it down to his vines in a measured prescription. 'Half a gallon an hour for five to eight hours every eight days.'

Too much irrigation brought bigger crops, fatter grapes, more juice, less skin. 'It's what a lot of people like, but not me. The wine has flavour, but no concentration. My ideal is small berries with a big ratio of skin to juice. My best Cabernet vines are fifteen years old – just half a ton of grapes to the acre in a good year, which is way low by industry standards, but it's what I like to see.'

Despite his high scores from Parker, he deprecated the trend towards Parker-style 'New World' wines – big and bold, all fruit and power. He wanted his own wines to have restraint, subtlety and the word he repeated several times, 'concentration'.

'How local is *terroir* here?' I said, swimming somewhat out of my depth. 'In a blind tasting, could you recognize the grapes from this vineyard from everyone else's?'

'I might have difficulty with Walla Walla Valley, but I could easily tell them from Yakima Valley, Columbia Gorge, or Horse Heaven Hills.' Each was a separate Columbia Valley appellation, or AVA, a federally licensed American Viticultural Area.

'And can you describe the taste?'

'Herb, with nuances of tobacco, berry and cassis.'

I wasn't sure if this was a straight answer, or if he was ribbing me for saying '*terroir*'. What I did cherish was his 'flavour without concentration' – a crisp, non-pseud description of a lot of wines I'd glugged down without much caring for.

No pesticides or herbicides touched his precious loess. Every terrace was hoed and weeded by hand. 'It's all about sustainability.' He was proud of the fact that he was now employing the sons of the

Hispanic men who'd worked for him when he first started the vineyard. 'Sustainability again.'

I was admiring his plantings of native shrubs, like juniper, on the land around the terraces. Everything fitted – this was landscape-farming that moulded itself closely to the shape of its original nature. 'It's perfect here,' I said, looking down over the valley to the forested Blue Mountains in the distance.

'I love this place's violent history,' Small said, meaning the lava surges and the catastrophic, Noachian flood that had swept through the Columbia Basin in the last ice age, some 13,000 years ago. The flood had been caused when a huge glacial lake in what is now Idaho and Montana had broken through the ice plug at its western end and poured into the basin as a racing wall of water nearly 1,000 feet high, scouring the valley to bare rock. It had left behind low hills in the shape of giant ripple marks, dry coulees, cataract cliffs and plunge basins, and the Martian 'Channeled Scablands' that had drawn NASA scientists here to investigate the terrain that the Vikings would meet when they touched down. It had also left behind Rick Small's favourite found object on his property, a lump of granite the size of a small chest of drawers. 'My erratic.'

The boulder had once been trapped inside a floating berg. When the flood receded and the ice melted, the alien granite found a home on Small's vineyard. One side was a sheer plane, the rock sliced through as cleanly as if it were cheese. 'See those scratches there, how straight they are? The ice did that. I had a geologist from the university come out here to look at it. He told me exactly where in Canada it came from. It's kind of inconvenient where it is, but I'd never move it It's part of the history of the land.'

At the north end of the vineyard, the rising, roller-coasting hills of sagebrush steppe went on for as far as one could see.

'So this was the last farm.'

'Oh, no, all this was wheat. Dry-farmed, no irrigation. It paid some years, but just about everybody went bust.' Pointing to the hills, he named the farmers.

I looked more closely, but couldn't see a single fence post trailing strands of rusting barbed wire. There were no collapsed barns or abandoned ploughs, nothing to suggest that here had once been homesteads, farm tracks, fields. No doubt a botanist would have corrected me, but all I saw was pure natural habitat, sage-grouse country, as it must have looked when the first white settlers showed up in the Walla Walla Valley.

If the market for perfectionist, expensively produced wines were to collapse, Rick Small's vineyard would fade back into the wild in the course of one generation, perhaps two. Hanford's plutonium factory will take a little longer only because of the toxic horrors buried in its grounds. From there, it needs no great exercise of the imagination to see the canals of the Columbia Plateau run dry and its mega-farms revert to sage.

Here's the difference between British and western American ways of seeing nature. Each time I drive through England on a visit, fresh blots on the landscape present themselves to my conventional eye: business parks, new estates, a motorway under construction, an expanded airport. But, as one does, I have a definite yet arbitrary line drawn in my mind between the undesirably modern and the immemorial. That line is recent – not much earlier than about 1900, or about the time the car arrived on the scene. A reflexive nostalgia for the antique is hardwired into my brain. Old stuff, however junky or ugly when it was first made, takes on value because of its age alone: the small thatched cottage with crooked windows, which began life as a miserable human sty, is a Grade II listed building now.

So I take indiscriminate pleasure in the packhorse bridge over the canal, the drystone wall, the field still marked by the medieval ridge-and-furrow system, the blackthorn hedge, the wooden stile, the now-dry communal village pump, the straight-line Roman road, the Neolithic tumulus, the one-track lane overarched by trees, the distant Victorian (or any other period's) spire – all equally immemorial and to be cherished because they represent ways of living on and changing the land that are all either long gone or as good as gone.

But here, where the lust for the antique is no less keen than in Britain, the true antiquity is wilderness. Old mining towns, chasing tourist dollars, deck themselves out with false storefronts, wooden boardwalks, faux shoot-'em-up saloons, but nobody's fooled. The real thing – the pricelessly *antique* antique – is deep forest, the river running wild, the open prairie. There is no second nature here to fall back on, only an either/or choice between nature as it was before we came and the dreck we've piled on it in the recent past.

In the dry and lightly populated West, for all the ranching, farming, logging, mining, damming and city-building that have gone on for the last century and a bit, for all the immense expenditure of public and private money lavished on its development, Americans have altered the land less immutably than the Romans, Saxons and Normans altered the face of England. Most of what has been done here still looks like a recent project, a work in early progress, that could yet be stopped.

In 1987, Frank and Deborah Popper of Rutgers University made a shocking proposal in a short article for *Planning* magazine, in which they suggested that the Great Plains, lying west of the 98th meridian and stretching from the Canadian border down to Texas and Colorado, should be returned to the buffalo. 'The small cities of the Plains will amount to urban islands in a shortgrass sea,' they wrote, calling their scheme 'Buffalo Commons'. The article was greeted with outrage by the Plains farmers. The Poppers were threatened with assassination (it didn't help that they came from, of all places, urban New Jersey). The idea was so extreme and sweeping that many people took it as a joke in bad taste. Yet twenty years later the article is still discussed, and the Poppers remain unrepentant. As rural depopulation continues on the Plains, especially in northern states such as the Dakotas and eastern Montana, they see their idea as being vindicated by history. In 2004, Frank Popper said that the article was originally meant as 'a metaphor for the environmental and ecological restoration of a lot of the Great Plains', and that he and his wife had been astonished by the enormous audience it had attracted. 'There is no question that some form of the Buffalo Commons will happen. We believe it is a done deal.'

That such a proposal could be entertained at all is a measure of how lightly white civilization still sits on nature in the interior West, how precarious is its tenure here. It's as if the land itself whispers that everything could be otherwise, that it's not too late to change, which is the vision that haunts the radical environmental movements.

Only in the West could one look at the Columbia Basin and so easily reshape it in one's mind's eye. Why not dynamite every dam on the Columbia and the Snake? Take down the power lines? Resettle the cities? Free the sturgeon and the salmon? Reopen the plateau to the elks and wolves? Farming would go on along the banks of the rivers, as it did before the federal government began to dream its grandiose dreams, but, for the most part, the land would soon go back to its immemorial state as sagebrush steppe, a tract of near-wilderness larger than any country in western Europe.

Of course it would wreck the US economy. It would send electricity prices rocketing, drive the local inhabitants to (probably armed) revolt, and mobilize the multinational agricultural and mining corporations to jam the courts with litigation for decades. The point is not that any of this is likely to happen, but that it's conceivable that it could. And people do conceive it, as the Poppers conceived the Buffalo Commons.

The idea of home as a temporary habitation is built into the folk psyche of the West. Most of the farmers who settled in eastern Montana and the western Dakotas in the teens of the twentieth century eventually starved out and moved on. Loggers and miners were itinerants, accustomed to striking camp every few months or years. Driving through the West, it's common to see houses mounted on the flatbeds of beflagged tractor-trailers, each off on a journey to a new site in another state.

In 1981, Norman Tebbit, then Mrs Thatcher's Secretary of State for Employment, caused an outcry when he told the jobless in the north of England to 'get on your bike' and look for work elsewhere. The remark deeply offended the instinctive English sense that attachment to one's place of birth and its known landscape and society is a moral right. People may move away of their own volition, but they cannot be cruelly ordered to get on their bikes.

It's different here, where people are in the habit of getting on their bikes many times in the course of their lives. One's local patch of soil is rarely an ancestral tenancy, going back through the generations, but rather a perch from which one may at almost any moment flit. That the demolition of the four dams on the lower Snake – an issue that's now being fought through the courts – would drive many farmers from their land is of no great concern to the conservation groups that have brought suit, because upping sticks and moving on has always been the way of the West. Let them be compensated, and go farm – if they must – somewhere else. *Get over it.*

So the hankering to wild the West persists, and I suppose that the project of restoring the Columbia Basin to nature would be hardly more gigantesque and unrealistic than the federal project of filling it with human population. For a start, one might post billboards around the perimeter of the Tri Cities (population 168,000) to remind everyone living there that, in the fine words of the Wilderness Act, man is a visitor who does not remain – the unsettling truth that westerners know already in their bones. ■

www.granta.com
Read an interview with Jonathan Raban

THE TREE OF THE CROSS

In search of the Fortingall Yew

Richard Mabey

S pending the first half of my life in the Chilterns, in southern England's chalk country, I grew up with yews. Not churchyard trees, but the bristly, mahogany-trunked nonconformists of the downs and beechwoods. They hunch among the grey-trunked beeches like dark Jack-in-the-Greens. Their seedlings, planted by thrushes, bristle impertinently on the hallowed chalk turf. Sometimes they grow into mature trees, but they never look old. They're short and stocky. Their trunks are nondescript. Every gale and lopped branch and suggestion of rot leaves its mark on old oaks and beeches, in extravagant bosses and flares of muscled lignin. But yews look impermeable, islands of mute shadow in the woods.

There was a yew in our parish churchyard in Berkhamsted, Hertfordshire, but it was a stripling, no more than 350 years old. It grew near the south-east corner of the church, on a mound that reputedly held the corpses of the town's plague victims. As children we'd dash over the mound for dares, risking the nemesis of a divine lightning strike. But I mostly remember our yew as a tree, not some austere symbol. It was a meeting place for revellers on New Year's Eve, and one wind-racked night I watched the thin twigs, as fluent as willow wands, blowing like black bunting over the crowds in the high street. Cults excepted, historical attitudes towards the yew were also secular, often matter of fact. The yew is an ancient British citizen, present here, give or take the odd ice age, for a couple of million years. Archaeological remains show that yews were widespread throughout Britain after the last glaciers retreated. Immense trunks and stumps have been discovered buried in the Fenland peat, drowned by the rising sea levels, in around 6,000 BC. Those on dry land began to vanish as soon as the first farmers arrived, doubtless hoicked out because their toxic foliage poisoned cattle and blotted out all life beneath. Reverence had its place, but not where a living had to be made.

The first truly ancient yew I saw was in Selborne in Hampshire when I was working on the biography of the village's most famous son, the naturalist Gilbert White. The Selborne Yew was a village landmark, but certainly not humbling or mystical or cathedral-like, or any of the other clichés that are used about old trees. It was not even particularly big, except for its huge girth (some twenty-eight feet when it was first measured), and grew modestly on the south-west side of the church. When Hieronymus Grimm made an engraving of it for the first edition of White's book *The Natural History and Antiquities of Selborne* in the 1780s, he pictured a distinctly stumpy growth, pollarded right back to the height of the surrounding cottages. In its supreme old age it was squat and fulsome, with the repose of a country alderman. What I loved most about it was the interior of the trunk. Old yews are almost invariably hollow, and the inside surfaces of the Selborne tree were patched with a satiny sheen of lilac and green and grey, like the lustre of mother-of-pearl.

This is my first time in the village of Fortingall, in Perthshire, Scotland, in what the local tourist board calls 'Big Tree Country'. The so-called 'Mother Tree', 250 years old and the ancestor of the 27 million larches that the Duke of Atholl planted across the local hills, is at Dunkeld, ten miles to the east. So is the Birnam Oak, the last remaining tree in Macbeth's mobile wood. The Fortingall Yew, which I've come to see, is reckoned by believers to be at least 5,000 years old, the oldest living thing in Europe. It was here before the making of Stonehenge and the Neolithic burial chamber at Maes Howe in the Orkneys.

The Great Yew is the supreme example of a mysterious conjunction whose full extent has only been realized in the last thirty years. Almost every one of Britain's ancient yews grows in a Christian churchyard, and almost all of them are vastly older than the church. The implications of this haven't been lost on modern pagans. The Fortingall Yew has become a 'Mother Tree' too, a 'Tree Goddess', revered by Druid revivalists, nostalgic wood-folk, patriotic Celts, even Christians with a strong sense of their church's roots. A florid New Age folklore has blossomed round it. Jesus visited it during his 'lost years'. Pontius Pilate played under it. A starburst of ley lines – from the holy isle of Iona to Montrose (Mount of the Rose), from Tobermory's Well of Mary to Marywell on the coast, from Eilean Isa (Island of Jesus) and Lindisfarne – converge at Fortingall, the *axis mundi* of alternative Scotland. Churchyard yews everywhere have been anatomized, blessed, danced round. Some acolytes see the species as the living type of Yggdrasil, the Norse 'World Tree'. A few have glimpsed in the Indo-European root of its name – 'iw' – a more than coincidental echo of 'Iawe', the Hebrew name for Jehovah, and have christened the yew 'The Lord's Own Tree'. Its timber has joined cedar, olive and elder as the wood of the Cross. It's a mighty weight of symbolism for a small and rather common tree to bear.

It's mid-March and the entire landscape is still brown tweed. Driving down Glen Lyon, with its hillside conifer plantations and bijou weekend cottages, I'm missing the sight of real trees. I know old yews well enough not to expect a skyscaper, but I'm looking forward to the tree frothing over the road, its spring shoots the first new green of the year. What I'm not prepared for when I finally arrive in Fortingall – an eight-hour journey north from my home in Norfolk – is the diminutive tuft, no taller than a teenage hawthorn, tucked under the lee of the Victorian church. Worse, the Great Yew is in a cage. This is to keep us, the restless public, out, not the tree in; at least that's the story on the noticeboard. When the yew was first 'discovered' in the mid-eighteenth century it was desecrated by souvenir hunters. They hacked pieces from the already collapsing trunk until it had effectively turned into two separate trees. By the end of the century, the gap between them was wide enough to carry a coffin through.

Squinting through the bars and reading the captions becomes, alas, the 'yew experience'. You feel voyeuristic, as if you're peering through a door-hole in Bedlam at an inmate slumped in the corner. The yew seems hunched as much by the enclosure as by its own ageing timber-frame. The northern half – a sheaf of knotted stems, each as thick as a sheep – has a few thinner branches that lope across the pen and stop dead at the fence. The southern trunks are propped up by crutches, and here and there by the wall itself. The interior is too dark to make out any of the exquisite texture you sometimes find in the interiors of ancient yews, and the trunks seem to be regressing to the quality of rock, not wood. But I can make out the circle of posts that have been hammered into the ground to trace out the original circumference. It was fifty-six feet. Twenty people could have joined hands round it.

I try gazing at the dim-lit scene as if it were a kind of sculptural installation. The last time I saw trees in a kind of cage was at an Andy Goldsworthy show in the Yorkshire Sculpture Park near Wakefield. He'd locked some dead oak trunks, stripped of bark and already as dark as coal, into a chamber of drystone walls inside a ha-ha, those picturesque ditches intended to blur the differences between the cultural and the 'natural'. When you peered down here, what you saw was not some panorama of the harmony of nature and art, but a vision of the forest cleared for – and handcuffed by – the walled field. Not an exhibit you would fancy joining hands around.

What shocks me now is how *dull* I find the Fortingall Yew. It has none of the panache and power and sheer narrative fascination of hardwood trees one twentieth its age. Yet as soon as I've made this admission, I realize how offensively human-centred it is. Of what possible relevance to the tree's existence is its visual appeal or intelligibility to human readers? Its capacity for survival is ultimately all that matters.

I walk off to the hotel (its bar is called 'The Ewe') along a series of paving stones spelling out what other beings might have passed by the oldest resident in Fortingall: STONE AGE MAN... PICTS... WOLVES... WARRIORS... ROMAN LEGIONS... WORSHIPPERS THROUGH THE AGES... AND YOU. It's another ghastly pun, but true. This commodification of an individual organism, this veneration of antiquity – which is only ancientness by comparison with our own brief span – is about *us*. The puzzles of ancient yews – were they sacred totems, planted by Neolithics? Were churches sited where trees already grew? – are seductive, but they are more about us than the yews. At Fortingall it is as if we can't see the yew except in our own attachments to it; as if we hope its origins, laid bare, might reveal lost human sensitivities. The tree itself, *for* itself, recedes, already resembling an inanimate standing stone, and not far off being the next piece of paving in the tourist trail.

Domestic animals apart, old trees are the only natural objects we view as individuals. In an essay titled 'On the Love of the Country'(1818), William Hazlitt wrote that our fondness for natural objects is distinguished by its 'abstractedness'. 'The interest we feel in human nature,' he suggests, 'is exclusive, and confined to the individual, the interest we feel in external nature is common, and transferable from one object to all others of the same class.' We still talk of hearing 'the' first cuckoo, that abstracted April clarion, not 'cuckoos', or a specific personalized cuckoo.

Trees had been noticed as individuals since the expansive days of the late seventeenth century. They were both ingredients of an increasingly respected nature and bits of real estate. As they aged they became not just more distinctive but positively monumental. They were status symbols, emblems of continuity. Big old trees consolidated place and the long span of history in a way that was rivalled only by big old houses. 'What can be more pleasant,' argued the agricultural writer John Worlidge, in 1699, 'than to have the bounds and limits of your own property preserved and continued from age to age by the testimony of such living and growing witnesses.' The big trees were pieces of property themselves, what would later come to be called 'heritage'. With an extraordinary presumptuousness they were often given human names. There is Wesley's Beech, Newton's Apple, any number of King's Oaks. I was once introduced to an 800-year-old oak in Dorset that was called Billy Wilkins after the local landowning family.

There aren't, to my knowledge, any named yews. Their brooding presence and toxic foliage didn't make them obvious candidates as either status symbols or ornaments. The realization that a few big ones had survived the millennia in the privileged environment of churchyards dawned in the mid-eighteenth century, when antiquarians were ransacking the landscape for any signs of an early and indigenous British culture. It was the beginning of a familiar process by which a wild organism is progressively de-natured. There have been claims and counter-claims about the meanings of the old yews, but they share one thing in common: the yew is seen as a human annexe, a benediction on humanity.

The Fortingall Yew was first measured by the naturalist Daines Barrington in 1769 at fifty-two feet in girth. Two years later his friend Thomas Pennant's tape showed fifty-six and a half feet, demonstrating how hard it is to measure these massy organisms precisely. The two men were correspondents of Gilbert White and had either prompted, or been prompted by, White's investigations into the tree in his own churchyard. White was aware it was a veteran, and thought it 'coeval with the church', the good Christian in him perhaps not ready for the implications of its being even older.

He assembled the possible explanations as to why there should be such trees in churchyards with his customary naturalist's thoroughness. He thought they might provide shade for 'the parishioners'; or a screen from the wind; or to provide faux palms for Eastertide; or to provide a reason to keep cattle out of the churchyard; or, most likely, 'as an emblem of mortality for their funereal appearance'. The favourite myth, in its pleasing blend of patriotism and whimsy, was that they had been grown to provide wood for longbows, which ignored the facts that English bows were made from the less brittle wood of Spanish and Italian yews, and that they were carved from the trunk, thus negating any other use for the tree.

This popularizing of the yew was done at a cost, especially for the Fortingall tree. In 1833, the antiquarian Dr Neil reported an early black market in Great Yew souvenirs. Bits of the tree had been cut away 'by the country people, with the view of forming quechs or drinking cups and other relics, which visitors were in the habit of purchasing'. Nineteenth-century Druid revivalists made a more thorough takeover. Although they had no objective evidence, they declared that the tree had been sacred to the cult, that it had been planted systematically around wells and other significant places, and that Christian churchyards associated with yews had been built on the sites of Druidic temples. Godfrey Higgins made the first claim that yews were Jehovah's own trees in *The Celtic Druids*, published in 1829. In *The Churchyard Yew and Immortality* (1946) the geographer Vaughan Cornish accepts that yew trees may have been sacred to early peoples in Britain, but that their evergreen foliage made them symbols of immortality, not mortality as White had thought. The Christian Church adopted them as symbols of everlasting life. Yet, confusingly, he also suggests that the planting of yews in churchyards was a custom brought here by the Normans, who had adopted the yew as a northern equivalent of the cypress.

Unlike earlier writers, Cornish had done his fieldwork. He'd written to every diocese in the country about their yews, and gone out to map a large number of them. The results seemed to prove his theory. Most of the very old yews appeared in territories in southern England and Wales affected by the spate of church-building that followed the Norman Conquest. And their positioning with respect to the church showed a surprising uniformity: most were on the south side, close to the door used by funeral processions. What Cornish would not accept was that the trees themselves were particularly old, living survivors of pre-Christian religious sites. The idea of a 2,000-year-old tree predating the spiritual founder of Western civilization was still thought to be blasphemous. As for the Fortingall Yew, there was a simple explanation for its longevity, according to the then director of Kew Gardens, Dr Edward Salisbury. The yew was not one tree, but two – or even several – fused together, an interpretation now easily shown up as false by DNA analysis of different parts of the trunk.

And there the matter might have ended, with the yews tidied away as a kind of pious bouquet planted at a church's founding, but for the intervention of Allen Meredith, an eccentric amateur historian with a touch of the wandering Celtic hedge-priest about him. Meredith had left school at fifteen with no qualifications, served in the Royal Green Jackets, lived rough for a while, been in trouble with the law. Then, in the mid-1970s, he had a series of mystical dreams, in which a group of hooded figures instructed him to seek 'the Tree of the Cross', which had a secret of profound importance for humankind's survival. For reasons he can't explain, Meredith interpreted 'the Tree' as the yew, and for the next decade he cycled around Britain, searching for the yew's 'secret'. He visited almost all the surviving ancient trees, measured them, probed deeper than anyone into historical archives and had more revelatory dreams.

He became convinced that the conventional wisdom about their ages was wrong by several orders of magnitude. He drew up a list of at least 500 yews in excess of 1,000 years old. At Ankerwyke, near Windsor, there's a yew with a girth of thirty-one feet which, he argued, was the tree under which the Magna Carta was signed; in Crowhurst, Surrey, there is a thirty-five-footer which he put at over

2,000 years old; in Discoed in Wales there is a tree much better preserved than the Fortingall Yew, but also, acording to Meredith, over 5,000 years old.

These ages can make you giddy, and incredulous. They far exceed those of any known oak trees, and most other species on the planet. And yews are all but impossible to date exactly. For their first 400 or 500 years they grow normally, if slowly, and they can be accurately dated by removing a thin core from the trunk and counting the annual rings. But after this their conventional growth slows down, and some actually shrink in girth for a while. They begin to shed their core wood. By the time they reach that potentially interesting and contentious threshhold of 1,000 years, they're usually quite hollow. Centuries' worth of early rings have vanished, and the tree has often begun bewildering growth spurts in quite different dimensions. It builds buttresses round the remaining trunk, plunging aerial roots down into the hollow. All orthodox approaches to ageing the trees – including carbon dating – falter when they arrive at an organic mass that is constantly reinventing itself.

The weight of Meredith's circumstantial evidence eventually led scientists to work out a tentative – though far from definitive – way of dating the old trees. It involved a formula relating the density of the rings in the outer wood to their distance from the centre of the tree, and it seemed to work quite well when tested on trees whose age was known from documentary records. When it was applied to more ancient specimens, it suggested that Meredith's informed guesses were broadly correct. The big yews were older than the churches, sometimes vastly so. This left matters deliciously unresolved, with the various theories now equally implausible. Could early church architects have so precisely oriented their buildings that they accommodated a large lump of still-growing timber just by the funeral entry door? Is the Celtic origin of yew-bound churches even credible, given that no archaeological evidence of underlying worship sites has ever been found? Is it probable that Neolithic peoples were deliberately planting a tree that grew of its own accord in the countryside around? If the yew really was sacred to them isn't it just as likely that they created their holy places next to existing *wild* trees?

There won't, I suspect, ever be answers to these questions. The quest for the secret of the yews is not an exercise in historical ecology, but a kind of spiritual geneaology, a yearning for Avalon, for the deciphering of a rune showing how we left the path of true religion.

In the meantime, the trees themselves continue to be just trees, showing reassuring signs of mortality. The Selborne Yew was blown down, aged approximately 1,500 years, in the great gale of January 25, 1990. The vicar gave a graphic and awestruck description: 'The massive trunk lay shattered across the church path and a disc of soil and roots stood vertically above a wide crater. The bench around the trunk was still in place, looking like a forgotten ornament on a Christmas tree. A stormy sea of twisted boughs and dark foliage covering the churchyard was pierced here and there by a white tombstone like a sinking ship.'

I'd gone down to Selborne immediately after the storm, and it was a scene of extraordinary activity. People from all over Britain who'd once lived in the village, done their courting under the tree, or just had their sandwiches there, came to pay their respects and beg or buy a piece of the wood. And still recovering from the devastation of the earlier hurricane in 1987, the local people were hatching a plan to rescue the tree.

By mid-February almost all the crown had been removed and things were ready for the Lazarus-raising. A time capsule (containing, among many other things, an edition of Gilbert White's book, with its early history of the tree) and a superfluous load of tree-planting compost were inserted in the root hole amid the resettled medieval skeletons, and a three-ton crane from the local agricultural college began to winch the bole upright. The children from the village school, led by the vicar, linked hands round the risen bole to pray for its survival. Stirred by all the activity, an underground main burst beneath the tree, and bathed its roots in municipal water for the next thirty-six hours. The tree was drowned where it stood. After a few months, during which it put out a number of new wispy shoots, the yew expired.

The village planted a cutting taken from it just a dozen yards away, but the fallow hulk lives on, in proxy at least. Its hollow shell has been colonized by young hazel and foxgloves, and a honeysuckle has wound its way up the headless trunk, like an Olympian victor's wreath. Bits of the pagan wood have found their way *into* the church, as a hanging cross and an altar screen.

Later that afternoon in Fortingall, I walk from the Ewe pub back to the yew. Its new shoots are foxy with pollen-heavy male flowers. It looks as if it could easily live another few thousand years, but only by becoming a kind of low hedge or rockery plant and abandoning the energy-expensive business of keeping a trunk alive. Beings in the natural world – trees especially – don't often cling to individuality in the way we want them to. Their boundaries become amorphous, absorbing and joining with other beings. The oldest living thing in Europe is not the Fortingall Yew, but almost any of the fungi that inhabit ancient woodland. They've been there since the woods sprang up 10,000 years ago, and their continuous underground tissue, stretching without obvious limits and entwined with the roots of most of the trees in the forest, is an immense single feeding cooperative which may weigh hundreds of tons.

On the far side of the yew, I find a stone in the wall, dedicated to a nineteenth-century incumbent of the church. A vigorous branch is beginning to overshadow it, and will doubtless soon be snipped back. One of the mechanisms by which yews extend their life is through the branches rooting where they touch the ground and sending up new trunks, which in turn send out new colonizing branches. The 'Mother Tree' survives by a dissolution of the self. It occurs to me that, without its cage, the yew might by now have loped as far as the door of the Ewe, in a thin green line of new incarnations. ∎

Gift subscription offer: take out an annual subscription as a gift and you will also receive a complimentary *Granta* special edition **MOLESKINE**® notebook

TEAR ALONG PERFORATION TO REMOVE

GIFT SUBSCRIPTION 1

Address:

TITLE: INITIAL: SURNAME:

ADDRESS:

POSTCODE:

TELEPHONE:

EMAIL:

GIFT SUBSCRIPTION 2

Address:

TITLE: INITIAL: SURNAME:

ADDRESS:

POSTCODE:

TELEPHONE:

EMAIL:

YOUR ADDRESS FOR BILLING

TITLE: INITIAL: SURNAME:

ADDRESS:

POSTCODE:

TELEPHONE: EMAIL:

NUMBER OF SUBSCRIPTIONS	DELIVERY REGION	PRICE	SAVINGS
☐	UK	£29.95	32%
☐	Europe	£35.95	18%
☐	Rest of World	£39.95	10%

I would like my subscription to start from: All prices include delivery

☐ the current issue   ☐ the next issue   GRANTA IS PUBLISHED QUARTERLY

PAYMENT DETAILS

☐ I enclose a cheque payable to '*Granta*' for £_____ for _____ subscriptions to *Granta*

☐ Please debit my ☐ MASTERCARD ☐ VISA ☐ AMEX for £_____ for _____ subscriptions

NUMBER ☐☐☐☐ ☐☐☐☐ ☐☐☐☐ ☐☐☐☐   SECURITY CODE ☐☐☐

EXPIRY DATE ☐☐ / ☐☐   SIGNED _____   DATE _____

☐ Please tick this box if you would like to receive special offers from *Granta*
☐ Please tick this box if you would like to receive offers from organizations selected by *Granta*

Please return this form to: Granta Subscriptions, PO Box 2068, Bushey, Herts, WD23 3ZF, UK, call Freephone 0500 004 033 or go to **www.granta.com**

Please quote the following promotion code when ordering online: GBIUK102

GRAPHIC FICTION

CLASSIC COMBO

David Heatley

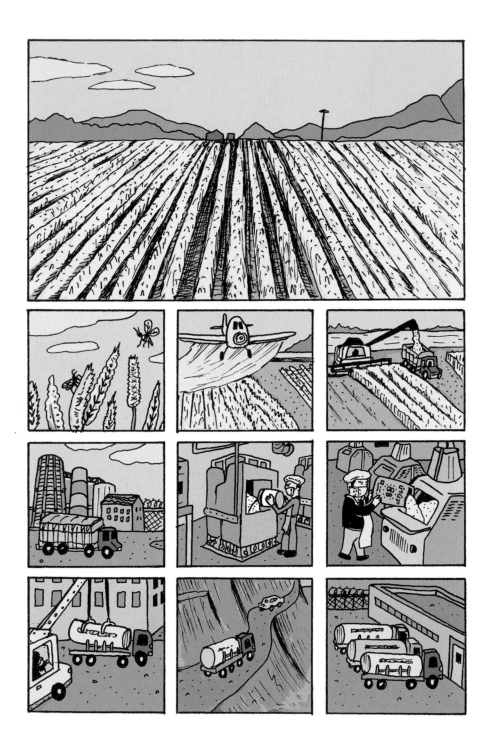

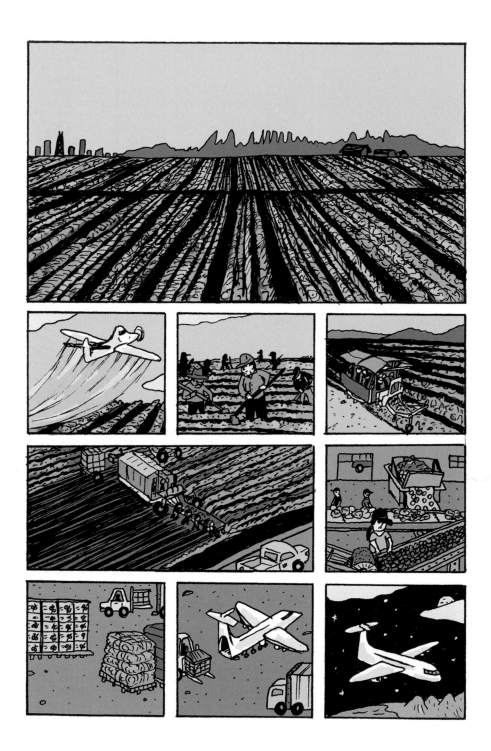

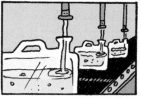

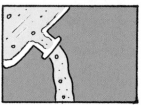

DAVID HEATLEY 2008

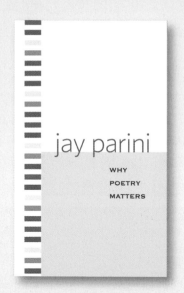

A brief, passionate book about the nature of poetry and its use in the world by award-winning novelist and poet Jay Parini. The author's love of poetry suffuses this book—a volume for all readers interested in a fresh introduction to the art that lies at the centre of western civilisation.

"With gentle insistence, Parini's book makes the case that poetry is worth reading—indeed, that it must be read—especially in a dark time like our own."
—Christopher Benfey, author of *Degas in New Orleans* and *The Great Wave*

224pp. £14.99

The National Gallery, London
Distributed by Yale University Press

In 2007, full-size colour replicas of 44 of the National Gallery's most famous paintings were hung—complete with frames and wall captions—on street walls throughout London. Recording this unique project and viewers' reactions to it, this book, like the touring exhibition itself, is a unique approach to looking at pictures. It also features photographs of the paintings taken by passers-by, unexpected and amusing comments from the London public and tourists and a foreword by Andrew Graham-Dixon.

96pp. 82 colour illus. Paperback £10.95

yale university press
tel: 020 7079 4900 • www.yalebooks.co.uk

FIELDWORK

GHOST SPECIES

Robert Macfarlane

Photographs by Justin Partyka

The ancient map-makers wrote across unexplored regions, 'Here are lions.' Across the villages of fishermen and turners of the earth, so different are these from us, we can write but one line that is certain, 'Here are ghosts'.

W. B. Yeats, *The Celtic Twilight*

On a cold morning last January, I travelled out to the Norfolk Fens to see a ghost. First, I caught a train twenty miles north from Cambridge to Littleport, a market town on the Cambridge–Norfolk border. At Littleport I was met by a friend called Justin Partyka, and Justin drove me in his little white baker's van up into the Fens proper.

Entering the Fens always feels like crossing a border into another world. Various signs mark out the transition. Ash gives way to willow. Phragmites reeds flock in the ditches, as do bulrushes. The landscape becomes rectilinear: ruler-straight roads and field edges, a skyline as flat as a spirit level, and on every horizon smart rows of poplar trees, planted to break the prevailing winds.

That morning, with the solstice only a fortnight past, the temperature lingered around freezing. The air smelt bright. Roadside rut-puddles were lidded with thin ice. An east wind was blowing, which set the dry reeds stirring and cussing in the ditches. We drove north-east along the River Ouse. Vast fields scrolled away to the horizon on either side of the road, most of them still bare of crops, but some furred with the green of winter wheat. Rooks wandered about on the loam, chakking to each other. One field we passed had been flooded and in the low sunlight it gleamed like a great sheet of iron.

Watching the landscape change around me, I felt a familiar sense of excitement: the excitement of leaving Cambridge behind and passing into a different realm. There are good historical precedents for such a sense. East Anglia has been considered its own demesne – separate culturally and geographically – for nearly 1,500 years. The region's name recalls the period from the sixth to the eleventh century when this bulgy peninsula was almost an independent kingdom: cut off from the rest of the country by swamp and sea to the north, the Midland hills to the west, and to the south by the wildwoods of hawthorn and blackthorn that reached up from what is now Essex.

I have lived in Cambridge, on the western brink of East Anglia, for about thirteen years now. It is a town that has almost no connection with the countryside that surrounds it. It sits as aloofly on its landscape as a bubble on grass. And for nearly a decade of these thirteen years, East Anglia was somewhere I avoided, on the presumption that its terrain held no interest for me. If I travelled in search of adventure or excitement in Britain, I always pushed north, away to the mountains and coasts of Cumbria, Northumberland and Scotland.

Over the past three or four years, however, I have begun to travel east instead of north from Cambridge. I've been to the salt marshes and mudflats of the Dengie Peninsula in Essex, where I spent a late-summer night sleeping out on the grassy sea wall, while hundreds of migrating geese barked and honked overhead in the darkness. To the Martian landscape of the north Norfolk coast, where the clear air plays tricks with perspective, so that thirty-foot-high dunes appear like mountain ranges. To the vulnerable coastline of Suffolk, where the sea is biting dozens more yards from the land each year and forcing the cliffs to yield up their contents: the bones of ancient dead, Second World War weaponry, Palaeolithic flint tools.

Once an anthropologist friend of mine, who specializes in the death rituals of Amazonian tribes, took me to the sandy ling-lands of north Suffolk, where two years previously he had buried the body of his father among the heather and rabbit warrens, before marking the site with a stone the size of a tortoise's shell. As we stood by the stone, my friend told me that he was planning to give the worms another two years before he dug up his father's skull, with a view to keeping it on his desk while he worked. 'I'll put a candle in it, I think,' he said to me. 'Or perhaps near it; perhaps just by the side of it.'

But the strangest of all these strange East Anglian subregions is undoubtedly the Fens. The Fens are a low-lying area of around 1,200 square miles in area. Geologically speaking, they are bounded to the west by the limestone hills of the Midlands, to the south and south-east by the chalk of Cambridgeshire and the sand of Suffolk, and elsewhere by the sea. To their immediate north, the east coast of England is punched inwards by the square fist of the Wash.

The Fens were once mostly water. In the ninth century, a Viking fleet could still sail as far inland as Ely. Until well into the 1600s, much of the Fens was a network of brackish swamps and reed beds, interspersed with islands and causeways of raised but marshy ground. The human inhabitants of this world were amphibious: travelling in punts, living in houses raised on stilts and surviving by fishing, cutting willow, reeds and peat, geese-keeping and wildfowling.

In the 1620s, however, the Dutch hydro-engineer Cornelius Vermuyden, already renowned for his success in dyking the Thames at Dagenham, was employed by the Duke of Bedford to turn the Fens 'into a sea of waving corn'. So began the draining of the Fens with davit, dyke and windmill: a process that would take more than 150 years, but which revealed hundreds of thousands of acres of the most voluptuously rich soil in England. A soil so fertile, Fen farmers say, that if you stoop and scoop up a handful you'll grow three more fingers before you've cast it down.

The Fens' terraqueous past is still visible in contemporary maps, most obviously in the generic names common in the region: the Sluices and the Bridges, the Lodes, Leams and Dykes, the Drains and the Mills. It is there, too, in place names such as Ely – which means 'island of the eels' – or Methwold Hythe: 'Hythe', from the Old English, meaning a small haven or landing-place on a river (visible too in London's Rotherhithe and Lambeth, which was once 'Lamb-Hithe'), though no river now flows through Methwold Hythe.

It was to Methwold Hythe that Justin and I were heading that morning. 'The Hythe', as the older people who live there call it, is an ancient village on the eastern edge of the Fens, just before the peat gives way to sand. In the late seventeenth century, after Vermuyden had done his work, a few miles' travel north and west would have taken you into the thick of the blue-black loamy Fens. But travelling a few miles east and south would have brought you into the Brecklands, England's Arabia Deserta, an area of caramel-coloured sand so extensive that an inland lighthouse was once erected to orient travellers, and so unstable that in 1688 a prolonged south-westerly wind caused the sand to form into a marching dune that buried a village and choked a river.

Justin knew Methwold Hythe very well, since he had been working there on and off for nearly a decade. Justin is a photographer who is fascinated by people of East Anglia – rabbit catchers, reed cutters, eel fishermen – whose rural ways of life have been brought to the brink of extinction by changes in the landscape. He calls them 'the forgotten people of the flatlands', though he also thinks of them as 'ghosts'. He has taken around 14,000 photographs, all on colour slide film; of these, he is satisfied with about eighty, and he is proud of perhaps a couple of dozen.

Among his different types of ghost, Justin is most interested in East Anglia's family farmers – the agrarianists and smallholders who still muddle by on a modest acreage. Until the twentieth century, the agrarian tradition in East Anglia was strong: thousands of family-owned farms existed, worked by people whose craft and local knowledge had been acquired over centuries and passed down through generations.

But then, in the first half of the 1900s, came the mechanization of British farming. The application of the internal combustion engine to agriculture meant that the horse was usurped by the tractor, that the boundaries of the village exploded and that the number of people required to work the land was enormously reduced. When the drive to maximize productivity began in the years before the Second World War, the flatness of East Anglia made it an ideal landscape for conversion to big-field or 'prairie' cultivation. Now, very few small farms are left in the Fens. Those that have survived are islanded by the landholdings of the mega-farms which now dominate. The rest have vanished: driven to extinction by competition with agribusiness, by the tangled demands of farming regulation, by climate change and by the lack of a younger generation willing to take over their running.

A mile or so west of Methwold Hythe, on Broad Drove, Justin stopped the van by a high hedge of hawthorn and ash trees. 'Let's walk from here,' he said. The wind was still strong, and it stunned the skin of my hands and face. I followed Justin down a muddy track, past a blue boiler-suited scarecrow that was sitting astride a rusty bicycle, and into a ramshackle farmyard. There were five big barns, a mobile home and a lean-to shed on to which twenty-four spanners had been screwed so that they spelled out A W VINCENT. Two of the barns were open-fronted and they were filled with a slew of objects: rusted pitchforks, seed drills, grease tins, pieces of timber, tyres, an old refrigerator and enamelled signs from the 1940s and 1950s

Sugar beet harvest, Norfolk, 2004

exhorting you to FEED YOUR DOG ON SHAPES! and BUY GOODYEAR: SIGNS OF THE TIMES! Nailed to the outside of one of the barns was a series of what looked like metal ribcages. They were, I realized, the latticed iron seats of old tractors and drill machines, polished to a shine by years of use. The only new thing in sight was a tractor: bright scarlet, black-wheeled and shiny. It seemed incongruous, like an outsize child's toy.

This was Severall's Farm, a twelve-acre smallholding farmed by Arthur Vincent and Henry Everett, both in their sixties. They knew Justin well and didn't mind him walking their land. Down by one of the stripfields, we found Arthur. He was pulling and banding leeks. 'Cold work,' he said. 'I used to swear I'd never be dealing with winter crops, only now I don't have a choice.'

'Just head on out, go where you want to,' he said, waving south. So we walked on, past a spear-forest of dead Jerusalem artichoke stems, ten feet high and bristling in the wind, and past a derelict barn – a 'tabernacle', in the language of the Fens – whose roof was being prised off by fingers of ivy. Past acres of muddy field containing stripped Brussels sprout stalks and smashed carrots.

Out by the southern hedge boundary of Severall's Farm, we discovered a rural riddle. Two blue plastic children's chairs had been placed facing one another, as though their occupants had once been in conversation. Nettles had grown into and through the lattice of the seats, binding them into place. Here, as at the tabernacle, the impression was of the wild Fen reasserting itself: fingers of vegetation reaching up to draw these human structures back down into the ground.

Near the chairs, we found a hole between two elder trees and ducked through it, then made our way north-east up the hedge line, into the wind and towards the Hythe itself. We flushed out a pair of deer and they raced off in synchronized bounds, before dropping down into the cover of a shallow dyke. The white winter sunlight lit up the east-facing sillion of the ploughed fields. I had the feeling that comes from keeping to the edges of an open landscape: hints of a

Eel catcher, Cambridgeshire, 2002

poacher's nerves; the excitement of concealment and faint subterfuge.

Away to our south, perhaps 300 yards across a field ploughed into corduroy lines, the field boundary was defined by a row of big old ash trees, their trunks and boughs shaggy with ivy. I thought of H.J. Massingham, the English writer who flourished between the two world wars, and who was, like Adrian Bell and Henry Williamson, motivated by an anxiety at the disappearance of rural English life. Massingham's response was a series of politically unsteady but often beautiful books about nature and the English countryside, which advocated the preservation of the social unit of village, of small-scale husbandry and of rural crafts and skills.

Massingham was an eccentric figure, and among his eccentricities was a loathing of ivy, whose presence he saw as a sign of uncared-for land. 'The axe,' he said of ivy, 'is the best approach to it', and he took to carrying a hatchet with him while he walked. In the end, however, it was ivy that did for Massingham. In 1952, out clearing ivy from trees near his garden, he fell on to a rusty scythe that was hidden in the undergrowth and wounded his leg. The wound turned septic, the leg had to be amputated and Massingham died soon afterwards.

After half a mile or so, Justin and I emerged from our hedgerow on to a rutted lane and brushed the twigs and leaves from our clothes and hair. From there, it was only a short distance into Methwold Hythe itself. Near the crossroads in the centre of the village, we turned left into a farmyard with a vast chalk-walled corn barn, its door propped shut with a fifteen-foot scaffold pole, and its red-tiled roof slowly caving in.

This was the Wortley farm, belonging to Eric Wortley and his identical twin sons, Peter and Stephen. It was Eric in particular that I had come to see. Justin knocked on a whitewashed door. 'Come in,' we heard a high voice cry, and Justin creaked the door open. I followed him into the kitchen, ducking my head under the lintel.

'That's a lazy wind,' said Eric, smiling. 'He never bothers going round you, just goes right on through you.' He was sitting by an old iron stove, whose belly glowed with orange embers. His legs were crossed and his hands clasped. Even in the low light of the kitchen, I could see the milky glaze of cataracts over his eyes.

Eric unclasped a hand and pointed to the empty chair pulled up tight against the stove. 'Sit down here by the fire, get yourselves warm.' Justin took a third chair from the kitchen table. We sat together quietly for a few moments, hands splayed towards the heat. A saucepan of water grumbled on top of the stove. A ginger-and-black cat was curled up on the brick ledge nearby, enjoying the warmth.

Eric is ninety-eight years old; Peter and Stephen are somewhere in their fifties. Between them Eric and his sons have put in more than 150 years of service on the farm. Eric is old enough that his early experiences on the land would not have been much different from those of someone who had grown up in the 1700s. No one knows quite how long a Wortley farm has been in the Hythe, but Wortley is accepted to be one of the most venerable names in the village. At present, though, with neither Peter nor Stephen married or with children, there is little prospect of the farm's survival. They are the last of their line: ghosts of a kind.

Eric tilted his head back and leaned towards me, trying to focus. 'These eyes of mine,' he said, regarding me with a grin, 'they're so smeary, they even make you look pretty. That's how bad they've got. Have you come far today, then?'

In a way I had come very far indeed. Only thirty miles or so from my own home; only thirty miles or so from Justin's. But to step into Eric's farm was to step back in time. Eric was born in 1910, in the house in which we were sitting. He had lived there for nearly a century, and the house had barely changed around him. Apart from a battered white electric hob and oven in the corner of the kitchen, little dated the room from after the First World War. Whitewashed walls yellowed by decades of stove smoke. A free-standing wooden dresser with wide eye-like cabinet windows. Gun hooks on the crooked ceiling beam of the room, from one of which hung Eric's

Eric Wortley, Norfolk, 2005

flat tweed cap, its rim and crown worn to a shine. A dark pinewood kitchen table.

'That's the same table I sat around as a boy,' said Eric. 'I was the eighth of twelve, not thirteen, because Mother had one that died when I was two year old. What was there? There was Dolly, John, Harry, Javie, Tom, Peggy, then me. I was eighth.' He half-sang this list of names, with the lilting Norfolk habit of prolonging and deepening the first syllable of a word, and shortening and heightening the second. 'And then there's Mary, Dick, Renie and Ted. That's how they was born. Every two year Mother had another one. Now I'm the only one alive out of them all. Whether I been lucky I don't know. Still, I've had a good life, I've always done my word and I've always kept here.'

Distance doesn't mean the same to Eric as to most other people. He lives in an unexpanded world. In ninety-eight years, he has barely left his parish. He has never gone to London. He has been twice to the Norfolk coast and once to Norwich, the county capital of Norfolk, about forty miles from the Hythe. At the end of the first afternoon I spent with Eric, a year or more ago, just before I got into my car to drive home, he asked me where I was returning to. 'Cambridge,' I said. 'Will you be able to get home tonight?' he enquired kindly. 'Won't you need a place to stay?'

Eric has exceptional kinds of local knowledge. He knows the water tables, the weather habits and the wind histories of every part of his parish. He holds in his head a detailed memory map of the surrounding landscape. He has walked, ridden and ploughed every foot of his land countless times, and watched its changes through decades as well as seasons. He knows the stories of the inhabitants, living and dead, and the species of bird and animal that have thrived or failed here throughout the twentieth century. And he has no interest in questions about the land that can be answered in the abstract.

The historian and folklorist George Ewart Evans regarded the elders of the East Anglian countryside as 'survivors from another era'. 'They belong,' he wrote in 1961, 'essentially to a culture that has extended in an unbroken line since at least the early Middle Ages... The sort of knowledge that is waiting to be taken down from the old people is always on the brink of extinction.' But, Evans asked, 'what is...the place of the small farmer in the new, evolving economy of today... Is there a future for him? Or are we to be reconciled to his extinction, attributing it to something that was as inevitable as a thunderstorm?'

Extinction presently seems inevitable. The Wortley farm, like almost all small farms in East Anglia, now exists on a diminishing island of habitat. Approaching Methwold Hythe, Justin and I had driven for miles through the land of the Shropshires, a mega-farm of over 12,000 acres. 'Shroppy's nearly swallowed us up!' Eric said to me that January afternoon, with indignation and a hint of pride that they hadn't been gulped. The scale of the Shropshires' operation is immense. Two years ago, when an unexpected May frost gripped the Fens, it was rumoured that they lost a million lettuces overnight.

Disappearance of all kinds preoccupies Eric. There is a spectral quality to his vision: he sees the past more naturally than he sees the present. The first time I went with Justin to visit him, on a hot August day, Eric took his stick from behind the door and walked us round his meadows, farm buildings and garden, talking all the while. I soon realized he was perceiving a different place from us: a farm where fences were mended, where pigs rooted in the straw, where the great chalk barn was uncracked and where horses grazed in the field behind the yard. 'Ah, you know, the boys don't see these things that I see,' he told me.

Listening to Eric talk that day, I was reminded of the evolutionary concept of 'ghost species', an idea that entered conservation science in the mid-1980s. A 'ghost' is a species that has been out-evolved by its environment, such that, while it continues to exist, it has little prospect of avoiding extinction. Ghosts endure only in what conservation scientists call 'non-viable populations'. They are the last of their lines.

The soft-shell sea turtle is a ghost. The desert bighorn is a ghost.

Abandoned farm, Norfolk, 2007

The tiger is a ghost, as is the sawfish. Show specimens of these species may live on in zoos, parks or aquaria, carefully curated, perpetuated through captive-breeding programmes. But hunting, habitat loss and pollution mean that, in the wild, these creatures have now passed into their spectral phases. Some of the most remarkable ghost species are to be found in the world's coral reefs. In those great stone cities are organisms about whose lives we know hardly anything and whose forms we can barely conceive of: the mountainous star coral or the Nassau grouper. Some of these creatures are angelic in their form, some demonic and none can exist outside the reef. They are almost all now ghosts, or near-ghosts, as the world's reefs are presently dying because of pollution, overfishing and, above all, the increasing acidification of the oceans. If the world's coral reefs are bleached into extinction, it will be the first time that human action has successfully annihilated an entire ecosystem.

The species most likely to become ghosts are those that are most place-faithful – which is to say, those that have evolved over long periods of time in response to the demands of a particular environment: reef, desert or jungle. Species whose specialized skills are not exportable beyond that environment and whose specialized needs cannot be satisfied elsewhere.

Historically, the idea of ghost species has been confined to the non-human kingdoms. But sitting in Eric's kitchen that January day, it seemed clear that there were also human ghosts: types of place-faithful people who had been out-evolved by their environments – and whose future disappearance was almost assured.

Eric, Justin and I talked on for two hours or so. Eric spoke often, and without sentiment, about what had vanished from the Hythe during the century he had known it: pipes and pipe-smoking, hedgerows, whistling and singing. 'We sung when we were following the horse,' he said, watching the stove. 'Or we whistled it on. They'd all be whistling then. Walking round, you'd hear whistling from everyone working on the land. You'd stop and have a little chat over the hedgerow. Nowadays you don't hear anybody whistle. It's all changed. It's a quieter life now, because nobody's on the fields. Everybody in the village worked on the farms. Everybody now, well, they leave the village to work. We all used to be a little family. Now I never speak to them.'

I asked him if the wildlife had changed. 'Ah, well, nowadays you don't see hardly no animals on the land. A hare or two, mebbe. No birds, hardly any birds. We used to have birds' eggses by the hundred in boot boxes, full of eggses. Kestrels' eggs, sparrowhawks' eggs. One of those was a white egg, another was a red egg – we'd climb up trees for them. A little old tomtit, a little jenny wren, could lay fifteen or eighteen eggs. We had names for all the birds. The thrush was a fulfa. Mabish meant mistlethrush, or maybe it was linnets. If you walked up to a hedge there'd be about twenty or thirty birds' nests about that time. They were thicker then, the birds. Tomtits, blue tits, jenny wrens, especially the jenny wrens. I don't see the wrens any more.'

The disappearance Eric doesn't tend to speak about, at least directly, is that of his wife, Ivy, who died in 1999, suffering from Alzheimer's disease. Towards the end of her life, her wits became so fuddled that she would often leave the farmhouse and walk out into the fields on her own. Once she left the house at night, and a police helicopter had to be called out to locate her. She was found sheltering in a small wood.

Midway through the afternoon, it became clear Eric was becoming tired. Justin and I stood to leave. He beckoned me over to his chair and put a hand on my arm, drawing me down. 'Remember this,' he said urgently and unexpectedly. 'If you've a good wife, it's a fine life! You tell your wife that, and you keep her, because, ah, it's a poor deal when she's gone. She was a Wren when I first met her, my wife, and she looked such a sight in her uniform! That was what won me, I tell you. I wrote to her, and she wrote back. At first we signed off 'Yours Faithfully', then 'Yours', then with crosses for kisses, and finally 'With Love', and that's how I did my wooing. All done by letter, my courting.' He paused.

'She was nine years younger than I was when I married her, and she's nine years dead now, and oh I miss her very much.' He peered away into the north-west corner of the kitchen. I could see the milky surface of his eyes very close to mine.

After we had left Eric, Justin suggested that we end the day with another walk. He parked near the beginning of a rutted drove road that led off, arrow-straight, to the south-west. We walked up it for a mile, past another tabernacle and a vast field of husky bean stems, and as we walked the weather shifted around us. High monotone clouds blackened the sky to our north. The sunlight became cold and blue: a storm light, whose twin effects were to give all standing water the appearance of zinc, and to lessen depth perception, such that every element in the landscape seemed to exist on a shared horizontal plane. Then a cold rainstorm blew in, belting big plump drops at us, and when we turned our backs to the rain we saw that a double rainbow was arching above a row of poplars.

And then, to our north, two dazzlingly white birds lifted off from a black field, instantly drawing the eye. The little egret used to be an exceptionally rare visitor to England. Then, in 1996, a pair bred in East Anglia; there are now around fifty breeding pairs resident in the region. Climate change has been an opportunity for this versatile species to increase its range, drawn across the Channel by the increasingly hot summers of southern England.

That afternoon, the appearance of the birds seemed like a surprising sign of hope: a new species making its home here, adapting to a changed environment. The egret is the whitest of any bird I have ever seen, perhaps the whitest of all birds. And in that storm light the pair condensed the sunshine to a magnesium-flare intensity. Justin and I watched as they beat away north on their wings, into the black sky, whiter than ghosts. ∎

---

www.granta.com
Read an interview with Robert Macfarlane

PHANTOM PAIN

Lydia Peelle

ILLUSTRATION BY TOM GAULD

S omething's out there. Something has shown up in the woods
of Highland City. Dave Hardy was the first to see it, the first
weekend of bow season, up in his grandfather's tree stand on the hill
behind Wal-Mart. Afterwards he bushwhacked hell-bent down to the
parking lot and, gasping for breath, tried to tell the story to anyone
who would listen. The story changed with the telling, and after a
while Dave Hardy himself didn't know what to believe: *See that old
pine tree over there? It was close to me as that tree. As close as that blue
Honda over there. As close as you to me.*

Panther. Painter. Puma. Cougar. Mountain lion. People started
talking. Word spread. Whatever you want to call it, by the end of
October, half a dozen more claimed they had caught a glimpse of it:
a pale shiver in the distance, a flash of fur through the trees. In the
woods, hunters linger in their tree stands, hoping they might be the
next. In the houses, the big cat creeps nightly, making the rounds of
dinner tables and dreams.

Twenty years in a taxidermy shop and Jack Wells has heard his share of tall tales, near misses, the one that got away. But the panther stories are different, told with pitch and fervour, a wild look in the eye. They don't carry much truck with Jack. No one, after all, has any sort of proof – a photo, a positively identifiable set of tracks, or even a really good look at the thing. For all Jack is concerned, it's an overgrown coyote, someone's German shepherd, or a figment of everyone's imagination. A mountain lion in Highland City? Sure, there's woods out there, hills with deep hollers and abandoned tobacco fields; not a whole lot of people, nothing to the south but the Plaxco plant, nothing to the north but Kentucky – but the chances are just as good you'll run into a woolly mammoth. People, if you ask Jack, have lost all sense.

His ex-wife Jeanne is the worst of them. Jabbering on about it like it's some kind of cuddly pussy cat.

'Oh, isn't it something!' she tells Jack, when they bump into one another in the frozen foods aisle of Tony's Shur-Save. 'Wouldn't I like to catch me a glimpse of it.'

Jack is on one of the store's motorized scooters, the basket filled with items he's begrudgingly picked from the doctor's new list: brown rice, cottage cheese, egg replacer. He's embarrassed by the scooter, and when he realizes Jeanne isn't going to say anything, he shifts around on the seat, boxed in by his shame.

'For Christ's sake, Jeanne. There's nothing out there.'

Jeanne lets go of her cart and puts her hands on her hips, cocks her head at him and gives him a look.

'And how do you know?'

'Because I seen everything that come out of these woods the last twenty years. Every buck, doe, weasel, turkey, tick and flea. There ain't no panther out there. There ain't been a panther for over ninety years.'

'Well,' Jeanne says, pursing her lips, considering this. 'There is now.'

At the end of the summer, just seven weeks ago, Jack lost his left leg at the knee, the latest battleground of his diabetes. He has only just returned to work full-time, and the walk-in freezer is stuffed with back orders: stiff red foxes stacked six deep and more buck head-and-shoulders than he cares to shake a stick at. Finished work crowds the shop: dozens of bucks, turkeys, coons, pheasants, squirrels on cured oak branches, large-mouth bass on maple plaques.

Ronnie, the latest in a long line of apprentices, still around only because he hasn't knocked up a girl or blown his face up cooking meth, sits just outside the walk-in in a ski parka, defrosting a marten skin with a hairdryer and grunting along to the radio. He came in three days a week and did prep work while Jack was recovering, leaving a pile of buck capes so sloppily fleshed out that Jack is having to go back over each one of them with a razor blade to get rid of the leftover bits of fat and vein. Jack is sitting at his workbench, shaking out a cramp in his hand and cursing the day Ronnie was born, when Jeanne comes in, the bell on the door jingling.

'Well, well, well,' Jack says to the full-body doe mount which stands next to him, ears pricked, front hoof raised, frozen in the moment just before flight. 'Don't look now.'

For twenty years, since Jack started the taxidermy business, Jeanne has come down to the shop from the house at least twice a day: in the morning to bring the sorted mail and in the evening to do the receipts and sweep. Four days a week she works down at the elementary school in the principal's office, a job she's had for forty years, since the summer after they got married. Jeanne kept the house in the divorce. Jack moved into a little trailer on what was left of his father's tobacco holdings, where he's been ever since. But his shop remained in their old two-car garage, a hundred yards down the hill from the house. It's a good spot – tucked up against a wooded hill, no neighbours for miles. He would never be able to rent a place like this, and even back then it had already become something of an institution among the men of Highland City. What he didn't anticipate was that the thin path that links the house to the shop would persist, worn down to the hard dirt through the years by his steps, now by Jeanne's. Jeanne does the ordering, the taxes, the books.

Ask Jack Wells how his ex-wife is and he'll shrug and roll his eyes and always give the same answer: 'Around.'

'All right, Hud, shoe off!' Jeanne claps her hands with cheerful authority. Once a week, for the six weeks he's been home since the surgery, she has insisted on cutting the toenails of Jack's good foot. This was how it started, on the other side: an ingrown toenail, a raging infection, his circulation shot to hell from the diabetes. Jeanne driving white-knuckled to the emergency room.

Jack throws down the buck cape and pushes his stool back with a screech.

'Where's the dog?'

He's peering into the open doorway behind her. Tiny, Jeanne's ancient and devoted black-and-tan beagle, was banished last week, after lifting his leg on a ruffed grouse.

'In the house. Don't you worry about him. I told him, I said, "Tiny, I'm not letting you out of my sight any more, you hear me?" '

She raises her voice an octave, to the sing-song tone she uses with the dog.

'No sir. Not with that mean old hungry panther prowling around here. Uh-uh. Not out of my sight.'

She takes off her windbreaker and lays it carefully between two raccoons, nostrils stuffed with cotton batting, drying on the plywood table in the middle of the room. 'Now, I want to get this over with just as much as you do, Huddie, so be a good boy and give me something for under my knees. These old bones can't take no more kneeling on concrete floors.'

As she struggles to her knees on his old corduroy jacket, he looks down at her. The top of her head is so familiar. The same perm she has always worn, only grey now, instead of red-brown: a black-and-white photo of her younger self. He feels a startling rise of anticipation for her warm, wet mouth, a forty-year-old memory stirred by the sight of her head at his lap: the back seat of his car at the drive-in. But then she pulls the little leather kit out of her sweatshirt pocket and unfolds it to reveal an array of cold, sharp metal tools, and he coughs and shifts his weight.

'Let's get this over with,' he barks.

Jeanne furrows her brow in concentration as she sets to work on each tough yellow nail. Jack folds his arms across his chest and puffs his cheeks, letting out a long breath. His stomach is bothering him. His stomach is always bothering him. It gurgles and spits, clenches and churns. Those pills. They gave him another set of prescriptions after this round in the hospital, after he made it through the unbearable days of physical therapy. He frowns and studies his gut, like a basketball under his shirt. He can't see beyond it to his foot, or to the metal rods of his prosthetic that peek out under his left cuff. In six weeks he goes back for the permanent one, the one that is supposed to be so lifelike he will forget it's not his.

'Betty Ann Flowers called last night. Her new miniature schnauzer? Missing. Disappeared clear out of her yard. That dog cost her four hundred dollars, too.' Jeanne draws in her breath. 'Can you even imagine? I told Tiny, I said, "Not out of my—" '

'Careful,' Jack snaps.

'I *am* being careful, Huddie,' Jeanne sighs. She can't understand why he doesn't see that this is all for his own good. He seems to think she wants to do this. She shoots him a look. His face, between the jowls, is the same as it has always been, like a familiar road widened for shoulders. She wonders if he is really watching his weight. He seems heavier. Her breath catches in her throat, and she looks back down quickly, telling herself not to worry about him. In high school, she'd thought he looked like – just a little bit like – Paul Newman. Not the eyes – Jack's were brown and sleepy – but in the chin, mostly. They saw *Hud* down at the drive in when they were first married, and she teasingly nicknamed him after the movie's cold-hearted, cheating hero. By the time the bad years rolled around, they were both so used to the name that neither one drew the connection, saw the irony.

*

CAT FEVER reads the headline of the *Highland City Gazette* on the first day of rifle season. There are two pictures below: a stock photograph of a mountain lion, teeth bared, ears pinned back, and a grainy photograph of Dave Hardy with another man Jack doesn't recognize, serious looks set on their faces, crouched next to a wash somewhere up in the woods. An inset shows what they are pointing to: a blurred set of tracks in the mud, which mysteriously disappear, according to the caption, after only a few feet.

'Could have been made by anything,' Jack tells Ronnie, peering down his nose at the paper. 'Coyote. Bobcat. Some little old dog. Listen. We just don't have the wilderness to hold an animal of that size. Scraggly third-growth hardwoods chopped up by logging roads and so full of hunters on ATVs it's a wonder they don't shoot each other's nuts off. A panther, first of all, is secretive and shy. Second, they can cover some ground. Fifteen, twenty miles a day. There just isn't the room. He'd keep bumping up against highways.'

'It's hogwash,' Jack tells Jeanne later, when she's down in the afternoon to sweep. The pain in his stump has been building all day, like a swarm of ants. He wants to go home and lie down in the dark and not have to see or talk to anyone for days. 'Where would it have come from in the first place? Closest it might have wandered in from, closest those things live to us, is the wildest bayous of Louisiana. You mean to tell me that a hundred-fifty-pound cat wandered out of some canebrake jungle, walked seven hundred miles without being sighted once, crossed four-lane roads and subdivisions and schoolyards and took up residence here? In Highland City?'

'Well,' Jeanne says quietly. 'You don't have to yell. And who knows? Maybe it didn't walk. Maybe it climbed up and fell asleep in a boxcar somewhere. Maybe it came on a train.'

Late on a Friday afternoon, Jack stops Ronnie as he's leaving the shop and asks if he's given any thought to his future. 'I'm not going to be at this forever, you know. If you put a little more into it, you could be taking over here in a couple of years.' But Ronnie doesn't think much about his future at all, at least not the kind measured in years. Ronnie has been thinking, lately, about quite a few other things. If he has enough credit to put a down payment on an ATV. If mountain lions are attracted to catnip. If he should ask his girlfriend, Tanya, to move in with him. Tanya is nineteen and a poet. Later that night, he picks her up at work and they drink beer over at Sullivan's. She sits across from him in their booth and scrawls in a big loose-leaf notebook while he watches a wrestling match on the TV above the bar. His sweatshirt and glasses are flecked with blood and bits of fatty tissue. Jack is always trying to get him to change his clothes when he leaves work. 'You can't be taking a girl on a date dressed like that!' But Tanya doesn't care, or at least has never said anything.

'You know what I wanna do?' he says, eyes on the screen. 'Get me one of them flat-screen TVs. One of them big ones.'

Tanya looks up at him, her pen in her mouth, and doesn't say a word. She is writing a poem about the panther. All her life, one thing has been sure: nothing ever happens in Highland City. Now this. She believes it is some sort of sign.

The feet contain a quarter of all the bones in the human body, the doctors told Jack when he was in the hospital: 107 or 109, depending on how you count a bone or bones of the inner ear. Either way, he is down to double digits now. He thinks about that often – too often. In bed, trying to sleep, he stuffs a pillow over the place where his left leg should be, the way the nurses showed him. When that does nothing to calm the pain, he lurches out of bed and finds the heaviest book in the house. When that doesn't work, he flings it across the room, pounds the mattress and bites the pillow. His leg. Sometimes he has a panicky thought that they gave it to Jeanne; in a jar, like a tonsil. And that she has it up there in the house, with all his things: his old records and taxidermy videos, the suit he wore at their wedding, his .22 and his mother's bible. All those other things he would have said twenty years ago were essential but had proven after all not to be.

*

Ray Blevins finds a dead fawn under his tree stand, all ripped to hell, half buried in the leaves, like something is planning to return for it. He comes up to the shop for no other reason than to tell this story to Jack. Ray is one that Jack has a hard time finding any respect for. One of the big talkers who needs a dozen technological gadgets to bring down a measly spike buck, who wants to go out there on a Saturday morning with his cellphone and his GPS system, his digital oestrus bleat call and human scent killer and $600 rifle and pretend he is Daniel Boone, out on the knife-edge of danger, deep in the uncharted wilderness. But a man couldn't get lost out there if he tried. That's why Jack quit hunting long ago, even before he got sick. Because you simply can't get lost and where's the excitement and pleasure in that?

'You know,' Ray says, jabbing his finger at the window, 'they say one of these cats will follow you. Read about a man out in Colorado got followed for twenty miles. They're just curious, though. Worst thing you can do is run. You run, then, well, kiss it goodbye. Get your jugular torn right out. If you know one's behind you, you just got to keep your cool, keep going on your business.'

Jack gives the clock a good long look, but Ray keeps going.

'Ten feet. Ten feet, they can pounce from a standstill. Tell that to your kid on his walk to school in the morning. Tell that to these people who think we should let this thing be.'

'Tell that to my ex-wife, then,' Jack says, turning away. 'She seems to think we should put a cosy little wicker basket and a scratching post out for it.'

Ray snorts. 'People just don't understand. What we have here, what we've got on our hands, is a monster.'

Those who have heard it say the call of a mountain lion is like the scream of a woman, more chilling – more hopeless – than anything you will hear in your life. The sound of a woman whose child has been wrenched from her arms, who is now watching, helplessly, as the last breath is choked out of it.

That no one in Highland City has heard such a night-ripping scream is one of the many points Jack constantly brings up in support of finding another explanation. What he does not tell anyone, not even Jeanne, is the sound that he himself heard, one night, a week ago, at the moment he had found a way to creep around the pain and part the curtains of a dream. Suddenly he was wide awake, terrified. *What was that? What the hell was that?*

But what with the painkillers he was still on. And the awful nights' sleep he's been having. Of course there's an explanation. It was nothing more than a terrible hallucination. And yet, for the past week he has kept the television on all night, the volume turned up loud. Just for company.

Ray Blevins buys a number-four steel bear trap with a two-foot drag chain and hauls a dead calf halfway up the hillside behind the filling station and when word gets out about it, all hell breaks loose. *We need to take action*, men start saying. *For the safety of our women and children. Before something happens that we all regret.*

Some Rotarians get together and invest in night-vision goggles and go out every midnight with an arsenal of rifles and don't come home until sunrise. Jack shakes his head and wonders how soon before someone gets himself shot. Whatever that thing might turn out to be, he thinks, why not just leave it the hell in peace? Every third customer who comes in asks if Jack will mount the cat for him if he bags it. And Jack, weary, counters with the oldest joke in the book: 'Sure, Bud. Two for one and we'll do your ex-wife too.' They slap him on the back, sending a tide of pain down his spine. 'Good one, Jack!' they all say.

One morning Ronnie grabs a pencil from Jack's workbench, draws something on the back of an envelope and thrusts it in front of Jack. He's breathing through his nose, his glasses slipped down, his flabby face trembling. 'I seen it,' he says. 'Out on the road last night. I seen it! Scared the shit out of me. Nearly wrecked.'

Jack squints at the picture: a primitive cave painting, a child's crayon drawing. 'You saw a water buffalo?'

Ronnie stares at him. He hits the paper with the end of the pencil. 'The cougar. Last night, around eleven. I was leaving Sullivan's. I caught it in my high beams, coming around that bend. It was there on the shoulder. Then it just disappeared into the trees. I pulled over but it was long gone.'

'You don't say.'

Jack considers the drawing again. It reminds him of the first couple of mounts Ronnie has attempted himself, a coon and a pintail duck: graceless, stiff, hastily and sloppily done. You have to lose yourself in the work, Jack has always believed. At some point in the process, even for a few minutes – and it sounds like a bunch of hocus-pocus – you have to let the animal lead you. After all, it's not clay or paint or iron you're working with. What you're working with has, up until recently, been a living, breathing thing; for a dozen years or more has been blinking, snorting, sleeping, grazing, scanning the horizon. You have to respect that. You have to get in touch with that, if you want to come close to reproducing it.

'Believe it now?' Ronnie says, striking the paper with the pencil.

'I'll believe it when I see it,' Jack says, feeling suddenly depressed. He's ready to go home, lie down on the couch, fry up a pork chop. To hell with his new diet.

'That bitch is mine,' Ronnie says, as if Jack has suggested otherwise. 'That son of a bitch is all mine.'

Up on the ridge under Ray Blevins's tree stand, the dead fawn's flesh is stripped away by coyote, then fox, then possum, their eyes glinting as they visit it in the night, tiny teeth tearing. The ants come too. Whatever killed it does not come back. Soon all that is left is the ribcage, looming on the hilltop like an empty basket.

One chilly December afternoon, the smell of snow in the air, Tanya comes to the shop to pick up Ronnie, whose truck isn't running again. Pulling into the drive, she sees Jeanne in the yard, fussing with her birdfeeders, squat and round in her big down parka, her glasses on a string around her neck. What is it with old people and birds? Tanya wonders. She thinks of her grandmother, the device she has with the microphone outside so she can sit in her living room and listen to the birds while she watches her soaps on television. If I ever end up like that, she thinks, climbing out of the car and skirting a puddle in the driveway. Stuck rotting away inside while the world goes on outside. Well, somebody just shoot me.

When Tanya comes in, Ronnie is working just outside the walk-in with a buck head that's hanging upside down on a heavy chain. He is slowly pulling the cape from the shoulders forward, until it hangs inside out, dangling from the end of the nose like a sock. Exposed is the gleaming naked head: white subcutaneous fat, blue and red veins, lidless, staring eye. Jack started the fleshing-out himself but didn't get past struggling with the winch. Now he's sitting at his workbench, hands on his knees, trying to catch his breath. He watches Tanya go straight over to Ronnie and lay in on him, their voices sharp across the shop. Jack is surprised and impressed at how she doesn't even take a second look at the buck – even Jeanne, after all these years, can't go near them when they're in this stage. After a few minutes she turns her back on Ronnie and, looking over at Jack, raises her hand to wave. He waves back. Suddenly she is next to him.

'Hey,' she says, almost flirtatious. 'Want to see my new tattoo?'

Before he can answer, she yanks the neck of her sweatshirt off her shoulder and turns around. On her shoulder blade, there are four short slash marks and a drop of ruby blood. At first Jack thinks it is a real wound. She lowers her voice and steals a glance at Ronnie, then levels her gaze at Jack.

'Ronnie thinks it's all a load of bull, but that panther is my totem animal. Want to know how I know? It came to me in a dream and told me so.'

Jack wishes there was some way to hide his heaving gut. 'You're going to have that the rest of your life.'

'Well, yeah.'

He's got one himself, from his stint in the army – a cloverleaf on his biceps, with his infantry division printed inside; they had all gotten the same one, one night in Texas. The colour is faded out now except the blue. What he really means to say – how can he explain it? The rest of your life, Tanya, is a hell of a lot longer than you think it will be. And you'll grow tired of everything. Your own face in the mirror. The sound of your own voice. And that's when you'll start regretting that tattoo. Not because you see it every day. But because you don't. Because you thought it would last forever, and remind you of something forever. And it doesn't.

On December 15, at one-thirty in the afternoon, Jack drives to the medical centre in Scottsville to be fitted with his permanent limb. He's rescheduled the appointment once already, dreading it, moaning about it for a week until Jeanne finally said, 'Oh, Hud! Grow up and just go!'

The nurse takes his blood pressure and vital signs as impersonally as if she's trussing a turkey, and shows him how to strap on the new limb. It is eerily lifelike, down to the wrinkles on the toes, and the exact same colour as his flesh. 'You'll forget it's not yours,' she says brightly. 'And, it's flame-resistant.' Jack scrolls through the possibilities for a wisecrack, but finds he simply doesn't have the energy. 'Fine,' he finally says. 'Good.'

The doctor is in and out in three minutes, barely raising his eyes from Jack's chart. 'Any questions?' he says as he goes, not leaving room for a 'yes'. He is already tucking his pen in his breast pocket, checking his watch and groping for the door handle behind him.

Jack is suddenly alone, left sitting on the table in his flimsy gown with a pamphlet in his hand – LIFE WITH YOUR NEW LIMB. It is filled with glossy photos of retirees acting like giddy teenagers: walking hand in hand on the beach, bowling, ballroom dancing – the woman with a rose clamped between her dentures. *Don't ever admit anything has changed*, they're screaming at him. *Never for a minute slow down or feel sorry for yourself. Look at us!* He crumples the pamphlet up and throws it in the trash can.

I do have a question, Doc, he thinks, sitting there, his shoulders hunched. Actually, I do. What the hell am I supposed to do now? There is something he hasn't had the nerve to tell anyone yet: he doesn't think he can go on with his work. He has never before realized how physical it is: the lifting, the sawing, six or seven solid hours on his feet – foot – a day. And it's not just the stump, the gone leg. He's exhausted to the core. Just yesterday he had to ask Ronnie to finish a coon for him – a simple little raccoon – he got so winded, trying to stretch the cape around the form. Somebody tell me what to do, he thinks, struggling to pull his pants on over the new limb, disgusted by it as if it's a bad joke, a gag trick. Somebody tell me just exactly what it is I'm supposed to do now.

On the way back to Highland City, Jack finds himself avoiding the rip and roar of the interstate. He takes the old road instead, the pike that stretches all the way up to Kentucky. It follows the natural valley of the hills and was the route the long hunters followed, two hundred years ago, when they came to these woods from the north to harvest the buffalo and deer. Jack's father used to tell him stories of the long hunters. They'd arrive with nothing but a gun and an axe, build a log cabin and stay for a year, eating deer meat and salting the skins, which they rolled up on a travois and brought home when they simply couldn't carry any more. Park-like forests, great open spaces under magnificently canopied trees. When the first of them came down from Kentucky, his father told him, they did not dismount, lest they be trampled, the woods were so crowded with game.

Jack tries to picture it, squinting up into the sparse trees on the hillside along the pike, but he can't. It must have been something like being in the shop, he decides. Big-antlered deer standing shoulder to shoulder, fox and weasel cheek by jowl. Except also wolf and bear. Mountain lion.

What if? Jack thinks, entering Highland City limits. What if there really is a mountain lion up there? The houses huddle on either side of the pike, brick and squat, with car ports and dog runs; the older ones at the edges of the last few tobacco fields, the farmers inside in front of their TVs, getting paid by Uncle Sam not to grow tobacco. He passes the gas stations, the cinder-block barbecue stand, the shopping centre, the new shopping centre. The smokestacks of the Plaxco plant poke up out of the hills to the north, crowned by white smoke.

If a panther really is up there, sniffing out an ancient path its great-great ancestors once followed; if, at this very moment, it is twitching its huge muscular tail and arching its back to run its claws down the trunk of a tree, dropping to all fours to nose at a beef jerky wrapper filled with dirty rainwater and picking its way around rusted old tin cans and television sets to make its way into one of those hollers, miaowing a lonely miaow – well, Jack thinks, pulling into his driveway and stopping to check the empty mailbox in front of his trailer – then I pity the old bastard.

Tanya, alone in Ronnie's house, takes off all her clothes and lies down on his new couch, staring at the blank space on the wall, cleared of posters to make room for the new TV. She's been driving back and forth to her place all day, bringing the last of her stuff over. Now she wishes it would all disappear. All those things that seemed so special when she bought them: her leather jacket, her laptop, her map-print shower curtain, her black boots, it all looks like a load of junk, now, stacked up in liquor boxes on Ronnie's kitchen floor. Moving in with Ronnie is the start of something, she knows, but she also knows that it is maybe not the start she was looking for. She closes her eyes and pictures herself hovering above all her possessions, flying away. She imagines herself in a forest. A dark, deep forest. Walking out into it, naked, and never coming back. She hears Ronnie fumble with his keys at the front door, swearing. She disappears into a cathedral of trees.

Tiny goes missing. Jeanne calls Jack late on a Sunday, apologizes if she's interrupting anything. He has been watching a tedious sitcom, his prosthetic off, the stump tucked away out of sight under a blanket. The bowl of chilli he spilled reaching for the phone is splattered all over the floor. He looks at it dolefully. Well, it was giving him heartburn and he shouldn't be eating that junk anyway. He pounds his chest and burps.

'Now, Huddie, I don't want to jump to no conclusions. But that cat, Hud – it could have just come down out of the woods behind the house and waited. I let him out for five minutes. *Five minutes.* That panther could have just slunk in and – oh! I've got goosebumps just thinking about it – carried him away.'

Jack can picture her perfectly, pacing the kitchen, ripping at her fingernails, the phone pinched under her chin. In moments of crisis, she has always managed to lose herself in a cyclone of panic. Never keeps her head. He sighs, too loudly, sending a rush of wind into the phone. Jeanne falls silent.

Damn, he thinks. Christ. Now I've done it.

'Well I'm sorry, Jack. I shouldn't have called you so late. I'm sorry. Never mind. Get back to what you were doing. Never mind me. We can talk in the morning.'

'We'll find him, Jeannie,' he hears himself saying, cutting her short. 'We'll find him. He's just gone off to sow some wild oats. He's just been feeling full of himself, these days.' As he goes on, Jack finds that he wants to believe himself. 'He just went off for a little tour of the neighbourhood. That's all, Jeannie. That's all. I promise. We'll find him tomorrow.'

When he walks into the shop in the morning Jeanne is there already, red-eyed and red-nosed, leaves clinging to her jeans where she's been down on her hands and knees, checking under the porch and in the old spring box. She takes a step towards him, as if she is going to fall into his arms, then hesitates, bites her lip, collapses in a chair and covers her face with her hands, letting out a muffled sob that hits Jack like a hammer in the chest. They drive around all day, doing twenty-five, Jeanne hanging half out the window, calling and whistling. *Tiiiii-ny!* It's a warm day, more September than

December, and clouds of hatched gnats hover in the road.

Jeanne calls herself hoarse. Every so often Jack finds himself looking at her heavy backside waggle as she strains out the window, then looks back quickly at the road, as if he's done something wrong. At four o'clock they decide it's time to quit, without having found hair or hide of Tiny.

When he drops Jeanne off back at the house, he grabs her hand before she gets out of the car and meets her eye. 'You gonna be all right tonight?'

She bites her lip and nods.

'You call me if you need anything. You just pick up the phone and call. I'll put the phone right by the bed. All right?' He watches her go in and waits until she's closed the door behind her before he puts the car in gear.

Jack stops at the end of the drive and pops a pill, eats a granola bar from the glovebox. He is cramped up, exhausted, the small of his back aching and his glucose levels all out of whack. He feels hollow, nearly desolate. It can't just be the damn dog, he thinks, driving home. It's something else, something bigger.

They'd driven down roads they hadn't been on in years – past the old empty high school and the field where the drive-in used to be, now grown over with highbush honeysuckle and littered with junk cars, a few speakers still hanging off their posts like rotted teeth. It looked like a war field. Finished.

He stops and buys a pack of cigarettes – to hell with it, he thinks, something else is going to quit long before my lungs do – aching for just some small physical pleasure to get him through the night. Before he leaves the gas station, though, feeling guilty, he shakes out three, leaving the rest of the pack on top of the trash can. Just as well, he thinks. Make some lucky sucker's day.

There is a place in Highland City that every generation thinks it is the first to discover, a glade-like swimming hole in the creek, set in a deep bowl of the hills. It's easy enough to get to from the road that you can bring coolers and lawn chairs and cases of beer, but secluded enough that you can do anything you want out there and nobody's going to bother you. When Jack and Jeanne were kids, everyone called it Valhalla, and spent their summer nights down there, when there wasn't something playing at the drive-in. I wonder what the kids call it now, Jack thinks, pulling into the rutted clearing off the side of the road. Probably nothing. These kids today have everything fed to them. No imagination.

Back in high school, Jeanne was always the first one in the water. Last one out, too. She was fearless then, even of the cottonmouths which scared everybody else off. She would stand in the creek, waist-deep, splashing the water with her fingertips. 'Jack! Jack!' she'd shout. 'Get in here. Get your ass down here!' He'd sit up on the bank with a beer and look at his friends. 'Already got him on a chain!' they'd snicker to one another, and Jack would do his best to laugh along with them, crack another beer and roll his eyes. He never went in, in order to prove something. Stupid reason not to go in, he thinks now. Should have.

He parks and pushes the seat all the way back, lights a cigarette. He closes his eyes, lets the smoke filter into his nostrils, along with Jeanne's familiar smell. He tries to imagine that she is still sitting next to him, eighteen and in a wet bikini, smoking a cigarette and playing with the radio. In those days there was always something good on the radio.

After a while, feeling stiff and caged in, Jack heaves himself out of the car and makes his way slowly into the trees, leaning hard on his cane. He starts down the hill, drawn by the smell of the leaves and the warm air that the woods still hold, and before he knows it, he can see the creek. It startles him. He makes his way down and sits with difficulty on an old stump to light his second cigarette. The banks of the creek are worn smooth from years of bare feet, littered with beer cans and busted sneakers and fast-food bags. On a beech tree on the opposite bank someone has spray-painted FUCK GOD.

He lets a drag linger in his lungs, feeling it creep in and fill all the corners. We had some days, he thinks. We did have some days.

Back when we thought it was all ours for the taking. Back before everything got ruined. And it all got ruined at once. Funny how it happened that way. Just woke up one morning and there was no going back and fixing anything.

A pair of crows takes off from a nearby tree, the branch shaking. There's a feeling at the back of Jack's neck like someone is behind him. He turns around twice, scanning the purple-lit trees. Something pops in his shoulder the second time, a painful little explosion of nerves.

Ghosts, he thinks, rubbing his neck. Ha. What ghosts would bother to haunt these woods? Our teenage selves. The long hunters. Not angry ghosts or vengeful. No, just – disappointed.

He shifts his weight and looks around for a grave. They're all over these woods. His father had taught him how to spot them: the depression in the ground that would be roughly the dimensions of a coffin, where the soil had settled over the years. 'Always watch out for them,' his father had said. Walking across them disrespected the dead.

The long hunters had buried each other in hollowed-out tree trunks, no time to build a proper coffin, no women to linger and weep over a grave. Scores of them must have died in these woods. A dangerous place, back then. But give me that over a hospital room any day, Jack thinks. And then, to be laid to rest the way so many creatures go: curled up in a log somewhere, tail over nose, and by spring they're crumbled into the log and the log, in a few years, is crumbled into the soil. It makes him feel cheated and lonesome, looking up into the leaves, the bare crowns lit with the last of the sun. There's not a single tree left out here that would be big enough to hold him.

'Take better care of yourself,' the doctor told him, 'and there's no reason why you shouldn't live another thirty years.' What the hell for? was Jack's first reaction. What's left? No grandbabies, no wife, no money to travel, and why did folks even bother to travel nowadays, when every place was just the same as the next?

Jeanne had wanted a baby. But those years, their chances, had disappeared in his drinking. I'm it, he thinks. The last of the Wells line. My work is all I'll leave the world. But some of the early work has already gone, popped at the seams, mice long since eaten the glue and made nests out of the stuffing. How long will the rest of it last? Longer. But not forever. For a while his mounts will hang in living rooms and hunting cabins and fathers will tell their sons, 'That's a Jack Wells mount. He was the best, you know,' but after a generation or so no one will remember his name. And a few more decades down the road, he thinks, at the rate we're screwing it all up, what will it even matter?

The sun disappears. It gets cold. Jack shivers and suddenly wants to be home. He looks at the hill with great apprehension and lights his last cigarette, hands shaky, wondering if his brain will be able to send the proper messages to his muscles to get him back up. Hell. So what if I die out here? He tosses his butt into the creek and watches it float away, the water rippling over the smooth stones of the bed, resigning himself to his fate.

But who is he kidding? He wouldn't die out here. He would just spend a cold, painful, sleepless night huddled under his jacket on the knobby roots and stones, and in the morning he'd have to piss on a rock, hobble up to the car, drive to the shop, take a dozen aspirin and explain himself to Jeanne, who'd have been up all night calling, worried sick.

Jeanne.

I'm going. Just as soon as I catch my breath.

A car pulls in up at the clearing then. The slam of doors. A radio. Kids. One of the voices breaks out from the crowd and carries down to the creek, a high manic laugh. Ronnie. Now I'm really going to have to explain myself, Jack thinks, but realizes that it's possible that in the dark they did not see his car parked on the other side of the clearing. Maybe he can get to it without them seeing him – if he skirts them and comes over the other side. 'Little punks,' he says, heaves himself up and starts up the hill.

But his body doesn't want to cooperate. His muscles bicker and then wail and scream. His good knee seizes up. Every few steps he leans on his cane and tries to reason with his thighs. A low branch slices across his forehead, stinging his eyes.

'All right now, Jack,' he tells himself, angry. 'This isn't Everest, you know.'

After what seems like hours he gets far enough up the hill that he can see the clearing, the light of a fire they've built. Six or seven figures huddled in a ring around it. He sees Ronnie, then Tanya. She's sitting off to the side, her hands pulled up into her sleeves, drinking a can of beer. The beer makes her look young, just a little girl. The group seems to be discussing something. But as he gets closer, there's a sudden shift. They fall silent, slowly put down their beers.

'Shhh,' he hears someone say. 'Did you hear that?'

'Listen. It's coming up from the creek.'

Tanya stands. Jack's heart swells a little, watching her, up there trying to see into the dark. Her face, lit by the fire, is filled with anticipation. Lips parted, her eyes dark in her pale face. Just pure and young and like anything might happen. She tucks her hair behind her ear and cocks her head.

Kids, Jack thinks again, fondly now. Suddenly he wants to speak to them, if they would only listen: I wish it was all going to turn out the way you think it will. I really do.

He lets a branch snap under his foot. That one's for you, Tanya, he thinks. A gift. He sees her raise her hand, tentatively, as if to steady something. She puts her finger to her lips. He smiles.

'It's...right...over...there,' someone hisses.

Ronnie stands up, poised, ready to run.

Jack gives the leaves a little rustle with his cane, forgetting the pain, starting to enjoy himself. And that's for you, Ronnie, you little SOB.

'That's it,' Ronnie says. 'I'm getting my gun.' He turns on his heel towards the truck.

Jack feels a chill of fear and takes a lurching step forward, about to shout, 'Don't shoot!' But then he freezes. He holds his breath. Jack hears it – whatever it is – Good Lord, he hears it, too. ∎

Abandoned flats at Tuffins Corner, Netherley Estate, Liverpool, 1985

NETHERLEY

Escaping the inner city

Paul Farley and Niall Griffiths

NIALL GRIFFITHS: Go to the city at the western edge of the country and then go to the edge of that city, the north-eastern edge, the very rim, beyond which you're not in Liverpool any more but Lancashire. The place is called Netherley, and it lies between Prescot, Knotty Ash, West Derby, and Knowsley; it's little more than a large housing project called the Woodlands Estate, abutting farmland.

I was brought up on that estate, from the age of around three to nine. So was Paul Farley, although I didn't know that until very recently, when we met for what I assumed was the first time in the Philharmonic pub in the city centre.

Which part of Liverpool are you from, Paul? I asked. *Estate on the outskirts. You wouldn't know it,* he said. *I might do. Try me.* And a couple of hours passed in reminiscence. *Remember the chippy? The white bridge?* Paul mentioned my brother's name, closer to himself in age. So we had to go back. I hadn't been there for thirty years.

PAUL FARLEY: Niall Griffiths's elder brother Tony was one of the kids I went egging with during the springs when I was ten, eleven, twelve. Thirty years later, Niall and I are rediscovering a childhood we didn't know we almost shared.

The night before we return, I parachute in using Google Earth: the planet, Europe, Britain, north-west England, Merseyside, and there, bulging out like a tiny hernia into the green, is the estate where we grew up, the circuitry of its streets and squares, the last place in an unbroken accretion that blooms outward in all directions like grey lichen from the mouth of the Mersey. I drop right down and steer by the main roads, hoping to recognize old haunts among the rooftops and car parks, fields and waste ground, the crowns of trees dark against olive greens and khakis. I struggle to make the imaginative shifts in scale, to put myself back in that time and place and to understand how, for fifteen years, this was my universe.

NG: The urban renewal strategy for Liverpool, which began in 1964, was initiated by William Sefton, Labour leader of Liverpool City Council in the 1960s and '70s. In effect, this would see huge areas of 'slum' housing cleared and 95,000 new dwellings built over a fifteen-year period, both in the limits of the city proper and on peripheral overspill estates. Over 78,000 buildings were to be demolished, more than seventy per cent of all dwellings in the inner-city area, thirty-six per cent of Liverpool's total housing stock. Prioritized in 1966 were the demolition of central slums and the construction of 32,000 new houses, both in the central belt and in the outlying areas of Netherley and Cantril Farm, to be completed in 1973 at a cost of £138,193,000.

Architectural blueprints were drafted according to the 'Camus' system of 'fully industrialized pre-fabricated systems of construction', which would see Liverpool overtake even London as a city of skyscrapers. Terraced rows were replaced by new blocks, both high- and low-rise, of flats and maisonettes, often adjacent – at Netherley, for example, off Brittage Brow, high-rise bulks cast shadows across the minnowed low-rise ranks at their footings.

Not any more, however; the high-rises met gelignite and the wrecking ball in the 1980s.

PF: It still feels like the end of the line. We're standing outside the parade of shops opposite the bus stop, wondering why there are hardly any people about on the street, why it's so quiet. My memories of this place are densely populated: of gangs at bus stops, of hanging round outside the off-licence, the chippy. Mr Walkers, the newsagent, a hunchbacked Yorkshireman who caught me stealing *Marvel* comics some time in the middle of the 1970s and told my father, who wiped the floor with me; the chandler's, which was really a hardware store, all galvanized mop buckets and mousetraps and that sad metallic smell, where we were sent for candles during the miners' strikes; the launderette, where I saw a boy shit into a top-loading dryer; Ernie the butcher, who paid me fifty pence at weekends to go into the bay at the back and break down boxes with a Stanley knife; the off-licence, or 'outdoor', ram-raided long before that phrase had entered the language; the cake shop, all iced buns and custard slices and things dusted with hundreds-and-thousands displayed on paper doilies.

Opposite these units there was also a haberdasher's we called the 'wool shop', a unisex hairdresser's, a bookmaker's (the 'betting shop') and the chippy, run by the long-suffering Mr Lau. There was even – and this seems so absurd now – a cylindrical advertising hoarding, a 'spinorama'. It must have cut a dash on the architect's maquette.

NG: Waiting at the bus stop, a teenage boy recognizes Paul. He attends Paul's old school, and has been given a collection of his poetry to read by his teacher, who also taught Paul. The boy is excited and exuberant; his enthusiasm is touching. Minutes earlier, Paul had told me how the flat landscape of the fields and barns over the brook had always evoked for him, when young, the works of the Dutch masters, an observation that he could never, then, share with his peers, for fear of indifference at best or some kind of punitive consequence at worst. Go from that to this boy, here, thrilled to meet a living, published poet, telling us about the millennium centre his school has built. Behind him, on a free-standing brick wall, reads the word SHEP. I remember that wall and that painted word. They've been there for more than three decades.

PF: The subway has been filled in. Half of the shops have not only closed but have been obliterated. Only the main parade survives, and there are two places open for business today. One is a general store on the site where the chandler's used to be.

I ask the woman serving, and she remembers names, places. We're about the same age, and so we're able to meet halfway by revisiting each shop in turn. *Mr Walker died years ago,* she says. His shop was being ransacked repeatedly, and he lived above, in a flat. One time the thieves smeared the steps with margarine so he couldn't get downstairs. He closed soon after, and she explains how, one by one, all the others pulled down their metal shutters for good. Whatever was fiery and vital about the place in memory seems long gone. It's like returning to an extinct volcano.

NG: The row of shops is now mostly a row of metal grilles. There's a small general store, surprisingly free of the shatterproof perspex shuttering around the counter so often seen in shops on these outlying estates, a hairdresser's and beautician's where the cake shop used to be, and the supermarket is now the Woodlands Christian Revival Centre.

The chandler's (not surprising that, even this far from the sea, there would be a chandler's in a city where the main road is the ocean, as one of its sons, Malcolm Lowry, said) is no more. The fish and chip shop is gone – flattened, obliterated, no trace of it, some scrubby grass in its place. A portion of chips from there used to cost five pence.

Sometimes, if we were persistent enough in our harassment, Mr Lau would chase us away shouting as he held a meat cleaver. The underpass which ran beneath it to the other half of the estate has been filled in. The off-licence too is closed. The Community Centre is still there, but its bingo nights have long gone; they died with Audrey, the organizer and caller, the sweet lady in the shop will tell us when we ask.

PF: A whole hidden economy flourished around here for a while. Mobile shops – essentially, the immobile shell of an old Luton or a caravan, even a shipping container would do – sprang up in every street, selling loose ciggies, milk, sweets: you could pay through the nose for the essentials. DO NOT ASK FOR TICK AS A PUNCH IN THE GOB OFTEN OFFENDS. Things came to your door: ciggies, booze, clothes.

Clothes were suddenly important. When I became a teenager in the summer of 1978, everybody was wearing tight Levi's; mohair jumpers were giving way to Slazenger and Pringle pullovers, Polyveldts or Kickers shoes, or their knock-off versions, bought from Great Homer Street market. Dunlop Green Flash plimsolls were re-whitened with house emulsion once they'd started to fade; fake Kickers leaf tags were cut from bus seats. The first silky synthetic sportswear was coming in – Le Coq Sportif, Sergio Tacchini – but the style hadn't settled into what was to become known much later as 'casual'. We were supremely faddy, and we were tribal. Clothes conferred insiderdom and belonging, and could mark you out from the kids off other estates. One winter there was a short-lived craze for wearing neoprene and Velcro windsurfing boots. I see myself, for the first time in decades, as one of a gang wearing windsurfing boots and deerstalker hats, walking through a concrete subway that isn't there any more.

NG: At the newsagent's, I would buy Letraset action transfers, favouring those that depicted dinosaurs or, for some reason, El Cid's battles. Such fun, calculating the scenarios, the control over the landscape, a positioning of paper and a quick scribble with a pencil and there it was, your idea of how things should be. There were abstruse skills to be developed; by hybridizing the kits, and with careful and selective partial rubbing of the figures on the transfer sheet, you could make a man's legs stick out of a tyrannosaur's roaring mouth.

Once, I took twenty pence into the newsagent's and attempted to buy four transfer kits; it was explained to me that, with each one costing twelve pence, I couldn't even afford two. *But I don't want two,* I said; *I want four.*

Why do I remember this incident? In such detail? The electric lights reflecting yellowly off the saleslady's lacquered hair. Her growing amused exasperation at my inability to grasp the maths. It didn't matter that I couldn't afford two because I wanted to buy four. I think, in the end, she put four pence of her own money into the till so that I could take home two.

PF: My family moved to Netherley at the beginning of the 1970s, part of a great wave of rehousing. I'd been born near the city centre of Liverpool and spent my earliest years living in Wavertree, in a terrace that backed on to the railway at Edge Hill. Both my parents' families lived in the streets close by. Then there were compulsory purchase orders and we were being shipped out to Netherley. Because they had four kids, a house was allocated to my parents (with a garden to follow), and I remember going with my mother to pick up the keys from a Portakabin. I ran through the new house, claiming 'my room' out of its echoey blank spaces, and am mugged again by its newness whenever I pass a building site nearly forty years later: the smells of raw timber, putty, wet cement and industrial adhesive transport me right back.

I can remember seeing all the old bits of furniture being carried from vans into these new, boxy flats and houses: dark-wood wardrobes and chests of drawers, sideboards, bow-fronted cabinets, radiograms, goose-neck lamps and mangles. Over the next few years, the back fields and lanes became littered with them, and the bonfires of those first autumns burned high.

But we'd carried our stories out here with us, too, and these proved more durable than the furniture we brought and the room dividers and fake-fire surrounds and white goods our parents went into debt for. They must have missed having an open fire. The houses had central heating, which meant a dull metal grille at ankle height in the living room, but soon anyone who could lay bricks and point found work building a fireplace for somebody. These become more ambitious as the decade wore on, room-length ranges with huge chimney breasts high as the ceiling, like something out of *The High Chaparral* or a Hammer horror, depending on the signature style of the brickie, and at their centre a fascia of plastic coals and logs.

NG: The urgent need for new housing resulted in a lack of municipal development, and on the Netherley estates there was a ten-year gap between the first wave of residents and the completion of the main shopping and leisure facilities. The few local shops that did exist often added a scarcity-value surcharge on to their goods, and public transport services were often substandard, reducing many lives to stultifying cycles of work and sleep.

Added to these problems was the quality of the housing itself: the Netherley high-rises were built cheaply, with linking decks between blocks saving on the number of lifts and staircases, making the project imposing and repetitive. The blocks were generally declared a mistake even before they were completed; the cluster of mid-rises quickly became known as Alcatraz. There was damp. Vermin. Poor systems of waste disposal and drainage. Concrete walkways and underpasses that seemed light and open in the airy offices of the planners proved dehumanizing and atomizing in hard practice. A poll revealed that, within the space of a decade, four out of five tenants desperately wanted to leave.

PF: In the 1980s, the estate achieved notoriety, a byword in the city for poverty, crime, addiction and squalor. In fact, its reputation attracted wider attention: Beryl Bainbridge visited in 1983 on the Merseyside leg of her *English Journey: Or the Road to Milton Keynes*

The white bridge

The row of shops opposite the bus stop

in Priestley's footsteps. If the Russians could see 'the infamous Netherly Estate [*sic*]', she wrote, 'the Eastern bloc would send food parcels and donations.' Magnum photographers Peter Marlow and Martin Parr produced images of dereliction and abandonment, ruined swing parks with climbing-frame ships emerging from the valley mist like the Fata Morgana, the deserted landings of flats barely a decade old. If they'd visited just a few years earlier or stayed longer, though, they'd have discovered a different place.

NG: Appleby Walk, that's where I lived. Next to Scafell Close, and other thoroughfares with Cumbria-referencing names. How are these things decided? To whom was such nomenclature an interesting idea? No high-rise blocks on this part of the estate, these are gridded terraces of five or six two-storey red-brick and slate homes built around central squares of grass which would be used as football pitches, often heavily fouled with dog shit. I remember running across one once, alone, late for the school bus, and tripping and falling face-first into a coil of cack.

PF: The place I point out to Niall bears little resemblance to the house where I grew up. But the estate always was a work in progress and by the time I left in the mid-1980s, a programme of demolition and rebuilding was already well under way. My walk to school took me through Brittage Brow, a canyon of damp and dangerous 'deck-access dwellings' (industrial, pre-assembled high-density housing) and I'd study the way the wrecking ball went about its business every day. Things were left abandoned for years, half finished. Roads seemed to change their minds and just stopped. Unpredictable foot-worn ribbons and diagonals soon cut across greens and along verges everywhere, what the urban geographers call 'desire paths'. Even language has proved provisional: the street names have been changed, the postcodes and house numbers shuffled. My childhood and adolescence took place on shifting sands: I watched it all go up, and I saw it all come down.

To some extent I must have absorbed and simply accepted this rate of change, but I wonder now how it was for my parents' generation; for those who'd grown up decades earlier within social networks and spaces where everything seemed to exist in a more reliable and recognizable relationship to everything else. Huge economic and social forces made and shaped places like this, then seemed to dump us here, sealed off from history, from our own pasts. There was nothing like a broad mix of social classes or incomes: all the people we knew were semi- or non-skilled, working class, and all of our fates were bound to the caprices of a shaky global market and a local economy that had yet to reinvent itself. I suppose I grew up surrounded by the ways in which the unlucky ones reacted badly, or didn't adapt, or failed to cope, drinking themselves stupid, damaging their families, hanging themselves from the cock loft. Many – my parents included – slowly turned inwards.

NG: It's cold today, and the frost that has carved the grass into grey lancets has yet to thaw. The goalposts painted on the gable end of Kirkbride Close have long been scrubbed away. We'd play 'shite' against that gable end, too; you'd take turns to kick a football against the wall and the other player would have to return the shot. Miss the wall once and you were awarded an 's'; miss again and you were given an 'h', and so on. It was best to blast the ball against the wall as hard as you could so your opponent would be more likely to miss the return and have to chase the ball. It must have been terrible for the residents of that house, but I remember being shocked and hurt when I was bellowed at by them; God, we were only having a kick-about. *Grumpy ahl get.*

PF: Niall remembers the white bridge too, and we walk down towards the woods that begin where the houses end, scrubby and dendritic after the rectilinear world we've just left. We talk about being on the very edge of the city, and I realize just how keenly I've felt that, even from an early age.

As a kid, I took the Cold War very personally, and would lie in bed at night worrying over the effects of an all-out nuclear strike on Liverpool. Perhaps the Russians wouldn't bother with us: I knew the seaport was in decline, not because I understood how gross tonnage had been in free fall since the 1960s, or how container trade had shifted to other, more profitable commercial hubs (in 1981, Felixstowe had become the country's biggest container port), but because my uncles and grandfather had stopped going to sea on the liners years before.

Still, I'd lie awake counting the blast rings. Ground zero was the Pier Head, the centre of a circle with a radius demarcating the edges of the city centre: total devastation. The second ring reached as far as the Picton Clock: widespread structural damage, fires, etc. Netherley, six miles out, was in a zone where there might be pockets of survival.

I must have been very taken with the acronym for Mutually Assured Destruction, because I wrote a poem in school that ended with the line, 'They're all fucking MAD.' I was sent to see the Head of English and didn't write a poem again for a long time.

NG: We cross the white bridge over Netherley Brook, at its junction with Mill Brook, a concrete and steel structure that spans a few feet of dirty water and under which, I thought, Gila monsters lived. I'd often take running leaps across the brook or the sluice gates – sewer jumping, it was called – or swing across it on a knotted rope tied to a tree branch. There were many fallings-in. The brook borders fields, across which we'd trespass, once to see a heron feeding at the pond; I can feel again the thrill as I watched it take off, pterodactyl-big, those huge beating wings, the ghostly silver and grey of its colouring. To keep us off the fields, farmers would often release bulls into them, or ferocious dogs, or, sometimes, load their shotguns with rock salt and shoot at us.

The woods hereabouts are today supposed to be junkie-haunted, but I see no evidence of that; no syringes, no burnt scraps of foil. Not even any empty bottles or cans. There's mud, and slime, and graffiti, and a not-quite-pleasant smell, but there are also many robins, thrushes and blue tits in the trees and I have no reason to suspect that the red-bellied sticklebacks I would see flashing with fire in the water are now gone. Water boatmen, too, their reflections on the muddy bed as if they were holding pompoms. The farm over the brook was a threatening and perilous place but there was magic on this side.

PF: The woods still feel like the brink, and the white bridge is like the border between us and another world. This was a prime hang-out, well away from the main road, and a good place to swig cider or smoke hash or sniff solvents. Beyond it lay open country, impossible places like Tarbock or Cronton where they spoke completely differently. Farmers were feared. Open country appealed, but was circumscribed by anxieties: hounds with mantrap jaws, bird-scarers, barbed wire. The urban had crept up on the rural and something of a siege mentality prevailed.

We were forever going on expeditions, sorties into a wilderness of drainage brooks, arable fields, sewage farms, disused railways: in today's *A–Z*s, the white pages, the blank edges.

This is where Tony Griffiths and I and scores of others raided the nests of blackbirds and dunnocks and song thrushes, building up our sense of what birders call 'the jizz': knowing a bird from a glimpse of its flight or a snatch of song, understanding its likely habitat. Skylarks were very common and we spent hours trying to find their eggs. The skylark was regarded as cunning, its song petering out as it dropped back to earth, always landing some distance away from its nest and scuttling along the ground to distract and confuse us.

NG: I remember it as an urban upbringing but it wasn't, really, and I'm startled, on this return journey, at the proximity of the green fields and the brooks and the copse of trees still standing, unconcreted. Netherley *feels* urban, undoubtedly, with the almost palpable pulse and pull of the big city a few miles away to the south, and images of the estate removed from the surrounding green belt would certainly suggest atypical inner-city housing developments, but I can remember a dawn chorus and can smell, here and now, cow dung and grass.

This is borderland, where the urban becomes the rural; the zone between ways of life, between specialized vocabularies, two localized lexica. As I recall, no one I knew had their place of work over the yard or so of sluggish brook; all worked in the city, or in the factories that lined the arterial roads into it, or down towards Speke or Garston or Halewood. The rural was there, close enough to smell, touch, taste; one bound over the brook or six paces over the bridge and you'd land in that world. Yet it remained very, very far away.

PF: We were great den builders, and for two or three summers dens were a huge part of my life; spaces cleared inside overgrown whitethorn hedges, fully carpeted with offcuts, furnished with pallets and those abandoned dark woods, ventilated to allow fire-setting. Some nights we'd go lamping with our neighbour Billy, who kept lurchers and Patterdale terriers.

Somebody discovered a Victorian dump on the town side of Netherley, and digging into its black oily earth littered with the broken clay pipes and Bovril jars and highly prized soda bottles from another age, I realized how this ground had once been deemed beyond the pale, a suitable site for the disposal of waste, out of sight and out of mind before the city had gradually caught up with its past. At that dump, in these fields and woods, we learned how to explore and find pleasure in our surroundings, and it feels to me now like the last moment when a generation of young lives could be lived largely out of doors.

NG: My mum and dad, they're up to something; they're giving each other glances, wordless and serious. They don't say much when we're eating, nor when we're sitting in front of the telly, but after a while my mum gives my dad a nod and he says, *Kids.*

We all turn to look at him.
How d'you fancy moving to Australia?
Netherley fell away for thirty years.

PF: Niall talks about how his father picked up on the estate's gradual change for the worse. He must have sensed it was going down the nick. Leaving at the age he did, I can't really talk to Niall about Netherley Comprehensive. It's difficult to describe the utter boredom I felt during my time there (I mostly remember it as waiting at a particularly dodgy bus stop for five years) and it's difficult trying to examine your own adolescence. I want to write that my sulkiness and increasing truculence and instability were mirrored by what was happening around me, but it must have all been so much more complicated. What I can say is that discovering art and books saved me from myself. The world didn't end at the white bridge.

NG: My family left the estate for Australia when I was still a child. Alcohol, and other drugs, would become illicit pleasures for me a few years after I left Netherley, but my secret vice growing up was found in books. Reading wasn't done. Reading wasn't for us. You were trying to be something you weren't, if you read. Ideas above your station. *Who do you think you are?* No house had books in it. No reading material of any sort, really, beyond the *Liverpool Echo*. Yet the culture was an oral one, with stories told and passed down, of the old countries, of wars. The power of words was acknowledged, and the thrill I'd get from encountering their written forms in jumble-sale books, read huddled and hidden in the woods or alone somewhere in the fields, blurs and becomes one with the happy shocks I'd glean from cider and amphetamine crouched in similar places in later years. This isn't a bad thing, for a confused child with a mischievous streak to associate reading with rebellion. In no way is this a bad thing.

PF: Were we always happy here? Niall remembers the violence of the place, its casual, routine cruelties. Dogfighting was rife. Every now and then, somebody would turn up with a ferocious new bull terrier that would wreak havoc with the local canine and feline population before vanishing as quickly as it had arrived. People gathered at this bus stop at night to watch 'the show', a demolition derby of stolen cars and handbrake turns.

It was a vulgar, brutal environment in many ways. Being spat on was normal. Faces were stoved in. A knife fight between two brothers ended with one of them bleeding to death outside the off-licence. My abiding sense is one of vigilance and a deeply ingrained wariness. Trouble would arrive suddenly, unexpected and grotesque.

One day in school, a lad I knew called my name down a corridor outside the music rooms; he kicked a ball towards me and I automatically received his pass, trapping it with my instep, but it was heavier than I'd expected, rock-hard underfoot, and it took a few stunned seconds for me to realize it was a pig's head.

NG: There was much cruelty to animals committed by children with gleeful sadism, indifference, or with a peculiar sense of duty. Water rats were pulped with stones or burst open with sticks. Baby birds and frogs were tied to fireworks. Nests were plundered of eggs and then 'scragged' – basically torn to bits.

Apart from egg collecting, peer pressure never affected me in this regard; I felt the same revulsion at such acts then as I do now. I recall a pet caterpillar popped open like bladderwrack between a bully's fingers. One boy turned a long flat pole – pointed at one end, forked at the other, and used to prop up washing lines – into a cat-killing spear; he hammered long nails through the pointed end, painted flames and forks of lightning on it, tasselled the other end with feathers, putting a high level of creativity into his cruelty. He'd hurl this weapon at cats and, if the initial strike didn't kill them outright, chop them in half with a spade.

Children made their own entertainment in those days. What's that boy doing now, I wonder? What kind of man has he become? Do those animals kick screeching and hissing into his present?

PF: Council estates are repositories of clichés, and one of these is the trope of escape. The bright disadvantaged child who realizes there must be something better and who overcomes all kinds of travails and adversities to find a way out, usually ending up in higher education. I suppose this is what happened to me, although I wouldn't ascribe too much will or determination to my younger self. I never found anybody else to share the thrill of paperbacks or the exotica of colour-plated art books with, and so for a long while I can remember leading a kind of double life, and might have settled for that.

And then a fluke.

Word got round that I was a good draughtsman and I started to draw for money. The people I'd grown up with had me painting their baby sons and daughters, their fighting dogs, their favourite album covers. Somebody said I should study art, so I took my work along to Mabel Fletcher Technical College in Smithdown Road and that really was the end of Netherley.

NG: Never entertain the notion for one second that in any way was it a bad place to spend most of a childhood. I left just as the desolation that would come with the Eighties was beginning to be felt, signalled by the thigh-high decorative brick walls around the green by the shops which were, overnight, smashed to utter rubble. The destruction of that decade had yet to be visited on the city, and outlying estates like Netherley would constitute the front line.

I would return to the city during the years of desperation, but to other, more central parts, when I would hear stories of the no-go areas of Netherley and the neighbouring projects, the robberies and stabbings and shootings and addictions. Bandit country, that kind of thing. *You were brought up there? Jesus Christ.* But it wasn't bad then. And it's not bad now.

PF: Another cliché: you never really leave. I lived in Netherley for far longer than I've lived anywhere else since, as if the escape velocity I somehow achieved has kept me moving right through my twenties and thirties. I've never known any other place so intimately, in such great detail, and it still feels like the last place I really, fully inhabited.

NG: Maybe we don't, can't, choose what to remember. Maybe we can't control what blunders and tumbles into our days. Because one of my clearest and earliest memories is of walking along a concrete embankment leading down to some garages and the sun was behind me, casting my shadow somewhat slanted and elongated across the concrete in front. It seemed a big and steep slope to me then, but I barely notice it now.

I was with my sister and my cousin and we were heading, probably, towards the woods and the brook; maybe I was going to show them where the Gila monsters lived. And the sun threw my shadow before me, long-limbed and angled obliquely, and I thought to myself, *It's a good job these two girls have a big boy like me to look after them.* I am five. ■

www.granta.com
See more of Paul Farley's photographs

Palestinian goat herders by the separation barrier

FIELDWORK

THE MIGRATION

In the skies above Israel and Palestine even
the movement of birds is controlled

Edward Platt

I

Yea, the stork in the heaven knoweth her appointed times; and the
turtle and the crane and the swallow observe the time of their
coming. *Jer.* 8: 7

Every spring, half a billion birds migrate through Israel and the
West Bank from their wintering grounds in Africa to their
breeding grounds in Europe, and every autumn they return the
same way. It's one of the busiest corridors for bird migration in the
world – only the Isthmus of Panama, which links North and South
America, has heavier traffic, and Panama's airspace doesn't support
the same density of military aircraft as Israel's. The large soaring birds
that migrate by day, to exploit the thermals rising from the land, pose
a particular threat to aviation: most of Europe's white storks and
white pelicans traverse the skies above Israel and Palestine twice a
year and, inevitably, collisions ensue. The effects of a ten-kilo bird
hitting a plane travelling at 1,000 kilometres per hour with the force

of one hundred tonnes are potentially catastrophic and, in the last forty years, the Israeli Air Force has lost more aircraft to 'bird strike' than it has to enemy action. Not surprisingly, it has therefore begun to take an active interest in the migration, and with the help of an academic and birdwatcher named Yossi Leshem, it has built a radar system designed to detect the passage of flocks through what it calls the 'bird plague zones' above Israel's narrow waist.

When I arrived in Israel earlier this year, I wanted to witness the spring migration and the military's attempts to monitor it, and I decided to go birdwatching with a Palestinian friend of mine. I met Sami Backleh on the second day of my trip, outside my hotel on the edge of Palestinian East Jerusalem. Sami became a birdwatcher by accident. He was working in the microbiology department at Birzeit University near Ramallah in September 2000, at the beginning of the second intifada. At the time, he knew nothing about birds, but he was interested in nature. One day a colleague mentioned that his son was working with an organization called the Palestine Wildlife Society (PWLS), which had set up a bird-ringing station in Jericho. When Sami went to visit it, he was intrigued by what he saw.

He must have made a good impression on the staff of the PWLS, for they kept 'nagging' him to join them. It wasn't a 'safe position' – he wasn't even sure that he'd be paid – but he decided to risk it, so at the height of the intifada, when Palestinian society was barely functioning, Sami began a new career as a birder. He treated it as 'an adventure', which became even more challenging when his colleague's son left after a month, leaving him to manage on his own. When Imad Atrash, the executive director of the PWLS, asked him to conduct a survey, he knew only two birds – the sparrow and the pigeon – and he was forced to teach himself by spending hours in the field with a book, identifying the different species.

In 2005, he came to England to take a degree in conservation biology. Nowadays, he is trying to raise funds for a project researching the impact of Israel's 'separation barrier' on the ecology of the West Bank. When work began on the barrier in June 2002, the government of Israel said it was designed to protect citizens from terrorist attack but, like most Palestinians, Sami rejects the idea that it's a security measure. He believes that the barrier is being used to appropriate land and natural resources.

Initially, the barrier was supposed to follow the route of the 'Green Line', agreed in the 1949 Armistice at the end of the war between the newly created state of Israel and its Arab neighbours, but it frequently deviates inside the Palestinian territory of the West Bank, effectively annexing parts of it. For most of its length, it consists of a fence, flanked by trenches, dirt paths and barbed-wire barriers, but in some areas it's a concrete wall, six to eight metres high. As well as dividing Palestinian farmers from their land, and imposing additional restrictions on the movement of the population, it's often said that the barrier is affecting animal migration and plant propagation. So far, approximately sixty per cent of the barrier has been built, and Sami is proposing to conduct a study of biodiversity in four sites in the same ecosystem, two on either side of the wall in the north, and two on either side of its proposed route in the south. It's a dangerous scheme: 'Imagine if you are beside a settlement, or beside the wall, doing animal trapping at night. You can easily be shot, and nobody will know. They will claim that you were a terrorist – that you were trying to climb the wall or something. So it's not easy. It's taking me a lot of time to select the site.'

We agreed to go birdwatching in the Wadi Qelt, near Jericho, ten days later, but as so often happens in the Middle East, events forced us to change our plans. At the end of the week, Israel launched an assault on Gaza intended to stop Palestinian militants firing rockets at Israeli towns in the south of the country. 'Operation Warm Winter', as the Israeli Defense Forces chose to call it, began with air strikes on 'terrorist infrastructure', but after two days, the army invaded northern Gaza and Mahmoud Abbas, the President of the Palestinian National Authority, announced that he was breaking off relations with Israel in protest. When I set off for Hebron on Sunday, March 1 there were strikes and demonstrations across the West Bank.

The next day, a twelve-year-old boy was killed in the village of Beit Awwa. By Wednesday, approximately 120 people had died in Gaza, many of them civilians, and at eight p.m. on Thursday, a van driver from East Jerusalem called Alaa Abu Dhein walked into the Mercaz HaRav seminary, the ideological birthplace of the Israeli settler movement, and shot eight students.

On Friday, March 6 Ehud Barak, the Minister of Defense, imposed further restrictions on travel in the West Bank, and Sami rang and cancelled our trip to the Wadi Qelt. As well as the difficulty of getting there, he was unwilling to run the risk of meeting settlers intent on exacting revenge for the terrible crime committed in an institution to which many of them look for guidance. I thought he was being overly cautious on my behalf until I heard that Imad Atrash, Sami's former boss, had also cancelled two field trips planned for the weekend. If I wanted to witness the spring migration in the skies above the West Bank, I would have to hire an Israeli guide.

We left Jerusalem at seven in the morning in a beaten-up four-wheel drive with 350,000 kilometres on the clock and no passenger seat in the front. I was sitting in the back behind my guide and driver for the day. Eran Banker was, like Sami Backleh, a biologist and birdwatcher. He was born in Israel, but had spent most of his childhood in South Africa. As a result, he saw himself as being at one remove from his compatriots, and yet he enjoyed the luxury that all Israelis share at home – relatively unimpeded travel.

Our first stop was the settlement of Kfar Adumim – the smaller neighbour of the fortified hilltop town of Ma'ale Adumim, which stretches deep into the West Bank. Eran said Kfar Adumim was a relaxed place, home to a 'heterogeneous population' of religious and non-religious Jews, and the guard on the gate waved us through with a cursory glance. In the past, I'd always stopped at checkpoints and bypassed settlements on my way from one Palestinian town and city to another. Now I was bypassing checkpoints, and stopping at the settlements, and so far I'd seen no evidence of the other inhabitants of the land, apart from the Bedouin encampments at the side of the road.

At eight a.m. we drove through the winding streets of Kfar Adumim until we came to an unfenced corner, facing east. The hilltop locations that the settlers colonize, for reasons of security, also provide excellent vantage points for birdwatching, and we were looking down on a series of interlocking valleys, which ran from north to south along the fringe of the Judaean Desert. It was March 10 and the hillsides were dusted with a thin green layer of vegetation. Soon the sun would burn it off, but while it lasted, it would provide vital fodder for the Bedouin flocks of sheep and goats, and fuel for migrating birds.

Eran set up the telescope in front of a bench decorated with a metal plaque. Swifts were circling in the valley below. They arrive in Israel and the West Bank in January or February and nest in cracks between the stones in the upper half of the Western Wall of the Temple in Jerusalem's Old City. I'd watched the dark flickering shapes wheeling above the bobbing heads of the assembled faithful at five o'clock one Friday afternoon, at the beginning of the Sabbath, and their movements had seemed as fluent and irresistible as the thoughts and longings that inspired the prayers written on pieces of paper and crammed into the cracks in the lower half of the wall.

We spotted a dark glossy bird, with red bands on its wings, called a Tristram's grackle, an iridescent, blue-black bird called the Palestine sunbird and a great grey shrike, or 'butcher bird', which kills lizards, mice and smaller birds, pinning the corpses to thorn bushes. Suddenly, the roar of engines shattered the early morning peace and a plane appeared from behind the houses of the settlement. It was a Hercules transport plane and its fuselage was painted the same dun green and brown as the landscape. It was flying so low that its bulbous belly seemed to brush the hills on the far side of the valley and its flight path and altitude told Eran one thing: the air force had received no reports of storks or cranes so far today.

Security precautions were more apparent at the next settlement. The guard on the gate at Mitzpe Jericho, which stands on one of the most easterly outcrops of the Judaean Hills, said that they had 'intelligence' of an impending attack in a stolen car or ambulance, though a brief conversation with Eran, in Hebrew, was enough to convince him that we were not terrorists in disguise. The settlement was enclosed within a high metal fence, and yet it was still expanding – as we left the last house behind and drove along a narrow ridge, we passed a group of caravans set up on a patch of scrubby land to the right. A young soldier was sitting on a deckchair in the shade of an army watchtower, a rifle slung across her lap.

The road ended at a fenced-in patch of semi-gravelled land with a black water tower. It was a place Eran knew well. Yossi Leshem's network of radar stations is not infallible (as Eran put it, Israel is so small that if someone burps in the north, you'll hear it on the border with Egypt) and sometimes southbound birds are over the centre of the country before the radar can pick them up. During the migration, human observers are required to augment the electronic surveillance and last autumn Eran spent ten hours a day, for two months, sitting on a chair by the edge of the cliff, counting the passage of raptors, cranes and storks.

The migration isn't the only attraction that draws birders to Israel – the country is approximately one-tenth of the size of the UK, and yet because of its location at the junction of three continents, it's home to a higher number of resident species. What's more, any bird that migrates even short distances in Africa, Europe or Asia can end up there by mistake. 'That's the magic that draws birders here – the great potential for surprises,' said Eran, as we stood by the fence sealing the sheer drop to the valley below. He pointed out a yellow-vented bulbul – one of the most common birds in Israel – and the rare long-billed pipit, and we heard a hoopoe calling for its mate.

We bypassed Jericho and headed north up the Jordan Valley, one of the northern reaches of the Syrian-African Rift which runs from

Turkey to Mozambique. It's a perfect avian flyway: its high sides and
deep centre generate the thermals that are vital to soaring birds
and its wetlands provide abundant food. We passed groves of date
palms and fields of cabbages and on the right-hand side, beyond
two parallel fences, the land fell away towards the Jordan river. The
border was no more than a shell shot away, and a decommissioned
tank dug in behind an earthen rampart, its barrel pointed eastwards,
commemorated former battles.

At twelve o'clock, we swept through the checkpoint marking the
northern limit of the West Bank and entered the Beit She'an Valley,
in northern Israel. The area is full of fish farms and its flat floor has
become a simulacrum of an estuary landscape. For twenty minutes,
we drove between thickly stocked pools and watched shore birds
– egrets, avocets, gulls and herons – stalking the fringes of the man-
made mud flats. The shotgun cartridges littering the paths proved
that this was yet another contested territory.

At half past twelve, Eran rang his contact in the Israeli Air Force.
The news was mixed – 8,000 white storks had taken off from a field
in north-west Israel an hour or so previously. They would be over
Lebanon before we could catch them, but another flock of 2,000
birds had been sighted an hour to the south, near Be'er Sheva in the
Negev Desert. We would have to wait to see which way they went.

Eran had left Israel when he was six, and he didn't return until he was
twenty. As a result, he had taken his degree when most of his
contemporaries were serving in the army; he did his national service
with people who were five or six years younger than him. Because of
a series of injuries he'd picked up playing sport, he wasn't considered
for active service and he had spent three years teaching children in
the West Bank about nature.

'I want my storks!' he said, when he rang for an update on the
birds' progress. The news was good – the flock had been sighted sixty
kilometres south-west of Beit She'an, and Eran reckoned that the
wind would push them eastwards as they travelled north. We set off

in search of a vantage point to await their arrival.

There were mustard plants and leggy yellow flowers called bishop's weed growing on the side of the road, and the hillsides were speckled with crown anemones and turban buttercups – bright red flowers which, to me, looked like poppies. Soon, the Haynes iris, for which Mount Gilboa is famous, would flower, turning the meadows purple. The wind was mottling the surface of the fish pools, and the haze was so thick that we could only just make out the outline of the Gilead mountains on the far side of the valley. Eran wasn't confident that we'd be able to spot our flock. 'Some days, you can watch thousands go past, and other days, you won't see anything,' he muttered as he set up our telescope by the side of the road. Earlier in the morning, he had defied a superstition by naming the bird he hoped to see, and *Merops orientalis* – the little green bee-eater – had rewarded him by failing to appear.

Fortunately, our white storks were less elusive. I don't find it easy spotting birds, even when they're pointed out to me. Often, the bird has gone before I've worked out where it is, but for once, I was looking in the right place. As I gazed at the crest of the hill to our right, a blizzard of dark dots appeared from behind it and swept towards us, moulding themselves to the slope stretching out into the plain. I checked my watch – it was ten past three – and when I looked up again, it took me a moment to relocate the birds. Already, they were in the middle of the valley, streaming out behind one another in a fluid formation, like a flattened speech balloon.

It was astonishing to think how far – and how fast – they had travelled. They had left southern Africa while I was still in England and, flying for an average of nine hours a day, at forty kilometres per hour, they had pushed through eastern Africa to their pre-wintering grounds in Sudan and Chad. From there, they turned north-west towards Egypt, following the Nile from Aswan to Qina, before crossing the Sinai peninsula and entering southern Israel. Only this morning, they had been in the vast expanse of the Negev Desert and now they were passing our station on the slopes of Mount Gilboa.

Eran lined up the telescope and stood back to let me use it. Its reach transformed the flock: it wasn't a blur of black dots any more. I could see distinct shapes, trailing long, collapsible legs. Their colour had changed as well. They were no longer black; they were white, with black stains on their wings. They caught a thermal rising from the slopes of the mountain and began to wheel and climb. At least 2,000, maybe more, Eran announced, adding with a touch of pride that he was a conservative counter; others would have put the number as high as 2,500.

Most of the hundreds of thousands of white storks that pass through the Beit She'an Valley stop to drink, but these birds wouldn't: with the wind driving them on, they would keep going until dark. They would roost in trees or on a cliff face, and feed on anything they could find – dead frogs, fish and insects. Sometimes, Eran said, they arrive in Israel with blackened legs and bodies, having scavenged through burnt undergrowth to feed on corpses barbecued in bush fires. By tomorrow, they would be over Lebanon and Syria, where they would turn north-west, cutting the corner of the Mediterranean and flying above the Turkish port of Iskenderum. They would cross the Bosporus at Istanbul, or the west side of the Sea of Marmara, and in Bulgaria, they would reach a turning point: some flocks would keep going into Central and Southern Europe and others would turn east, towards nesting grounds in western Russia.

I looked up again, wanting to place them in the broader context of the valley, but I couldn't find them. This time, Eran had lost them too. He was scanning the horizon with binoculars, but already the birds had disappeared.

II

And the word of the Lord came unto him, saying, Get thee hence, and turn thee eastward, and hide thyself by the brook Cherith, that is before Jordan. And it shall be, that thou shalt drink of the brook; and I have commanded the ravens to feed thee there. 1 *Kings* 17: 2 – 4

The most common migratory bird in the Middle East is a sylviid warbler called the blackcap. Like all the passerines or songbirds that pass through the region, it travels at night, when it's cooler and there are fewer predators around, and it flies by flapping its wings as opposed to relying on updrafts. Since it winters in northern Africa and summers in Germany, it travels a shorter distance than the white stork, and yet its journey is a remarkable feat of endurance. Normally, it weighs twelve grams, the same as a two-pound coin, but it will double in weight before it embarks on its migration. When it arrives in southern Israel, at the end of its desert crossing, it will have burnt up the extra fat, and more. According to Amir Balaban, one of the directors of the Jerusalem Bird Observatory (JBO), it will be thin and exhausted, and will rest and feed at an oasis in Elat or the Arava Valley before it resumes its journey.

Since the Jerusalem region lies within the most southerly reaches of the Mediterranean habitat, many of the birds aim for it, and the JBO, in the heart of the government district to the west of the city, is a particularly important stopping-off point. On the morning I visited, they had caught four blackcaps in the nets slung between the trees and in April, when the migration is in full flood, they will catch as many as fifty a day.

Four days had passed since my trip along the Rift Valley with Eran Banker. It was the Sabbath and when the taxi dropped me opposite the Supreme Court at seven-thirty, there was no one – other than Amir Balaban – around. He was planting a shrub beside a reed-fringed pond to the side of the path that led to the carefully cultivated wilderness of the observatory. He's a stocky man with close-cropped hair and he was dressed in the uniform of birders and outdoor-lovers throughout the Western world – pale walking trousers, a fleece and sandals. We moved to the hide and sat looking out through the narrow slit at the birds gathering on the feeding table and the fringes of the pond. Through the trees, we could see the high-rise towers of the suburb of Nahlaot, which was founded in the nineteenth century by Jews escaping the cramped confines of the Old City.

The area had once been farmland belonging to an Arab village that was destroyed in the war of 1947–8, when the fledgling Israeli state was attempting to retain, and expand, the territory it had been allotted in the UN plan to partition Palestine. According to some estimates, as many as 400 villages were decimated in the course of the war and approximately 700,000 people were forced to leave their homes. The Palestinians call the mass exodus the *nakba*, or 'catastrophe', though not surprisingly, the Israelis have a different name for the events of the year – the graveyard abutting the JBO's borders is largely devoted to people killed in 'the War of Independence'.

In 1966 the Knesset, the parliament of Israel, moved to its current home from temporary lodgings in King George Street and, for the next twenty years or so, the land was used as an 'organic rubbish dump'. Amir Balaban began birdwatching as a child among its dense, untended shrubs and trees, and in 1994, the Knesset was persuaded to lease the site to the JBO. Amir believes that its location is significant, because it asserts the primacy of nature and wildlife in Israeli life. He believes it's the organization's job to make sure that the half a billion birds that pass through the region each spring do so safely, and yet given the proportion of bird-lovers to bird-hunters in every country in the Mediterranean region – from France, Italy, Malta, Greece and Turkey to Lebanon, Syria, Egypt, Tunisia, Libya and Morocco – their task is difficult.

The JBO was the first ringing station in the Middle East; the bird-ringers who established the Jericho station where Sami worked were trained here. Amir told me that a shared passion for birds and wildlife will overcome most difficulties, 'political or ideological', but he was realistic about the relationship between the birdwatchers on either side of the divide: 'We do have our...*disagreements* with our Palestinian friends.' He chose the word carefully.

I still wanted to witness the migration from the Palestinian perspective and when I left the JBO, I called Imad Atrash. In the next few days, we arranged to meet several times, but without success.

One morning, I stood outside the police station in Bethlehem's Manger Square for an hour and a half, waiting for his 'driver', who failed to appear, despite Imad's repeated assurances that he was on his way. I found it hard to conceal my irritation, though I had to remind myself that it's difficult to maintain normal standards of efficiency when you're living under occupation. I was beginning to think that we were never going to meet when he rang three days before the end of my trip and invited me to Jericho.

We met outside the municipality building and drove into the hills through a small village called Jericho's Gate. There were children playing by the side of the road, and I saw a young boy climbing past a roll of barbed wire. On the edges of the town, the road grew steeper and narrower. Soon, we were running along the edge of a deep ravine. Imad called it Palestine's Grand Canyon, though it's better known as the Wadi Qelt. I'd hoped to walk through it from the west, and I hadn't expected to find myself driving in from the other direction.

The dark red cliffs were striped with horizontal fissures and beyond them the pale, mounded hills looked as if they were made of poured concrete. Jericho was spreading out beneath us, and it looked surprisingly green, like a pool of emerald water gathered in a dip in the desert.

Imad was driving and his researcher was sitting in the front seat. The car's wheels were no more than a couple of feet from the edge of the cliff. He caught my eye in the rear-view mirror.

'Are you afraid?'

'A little.'

'You needn't be afraid with Imad Atrash.'

The road began to descend again, and we drew up in front of a roadblock made of concrete blocks driven into mounds of rubble. Sami's fears had been justified: there had been a fight between Palestinians and settlers from Vered Jericho on the day that we had planned our walk, and the army had sealed, or resealed, the road between the settlement and the town.

We followed a path that wound through the lunar strip and emerged on an area of smooth, dark tarmac, opposite a large stone arch, surmounted by a cross. We had a choice of two paths: the first led through the arch and fell sharply downwards, but we took the other one leading upwards and came to a vantage point on the cliff top. Beneath us, tucked into a platform against the cliff face on the far side of the valley, was the monastery of St George.

The road we hadn't taken emerged at the base of the cliff and ran through the bottom of the valley. It crossed a bridge and led to a gatehouse adorned with a red cross on a white background. Beyond it, steps led up to another wall and a steep tower, crowned with a sky-blue dome. A culvert filled with water ran beside the road at the bottom of the valley, and the lower slopes of the hills were lush and green. Some people believe that 'the brook Cherith, that is before Jordan' is the Wadi Qelt, and the monastery is supposed to have been founded in AD 420 by five hermits, next to the cave where Elijah was fed by ravens when he fled Israel to avoid a drought. When the Persians conquered Palestine in the seventh century, they massacred fourteen monks, whose bones are preserved in a cave near the monastery. The monastery was subsequently abandoned, but it was restored by the Crusaders in 1179, and rebuilt at the beginning of the twentieth century by the Greek Orthodox Church.

Over the years, many cave-dwelling hermits have lived in the Wadi Qelt in imitation of Elijah, and the cliff face above the monastery is pocked with caves still used by the monks as places of retreat. There were crosses on every hilltop as far as I could see and in the distance we could make out the antenna of the radar station on the summit of the Mount of Temptation.

Imad had set up his telescope on the edge of the cliff. I assumed that he was watching for birds but in fact he had spotted someone in the courtyard of the monastery. He looked up from the telescope: 'Abu Majid!' His booming voice echoed around the walls of the canyon. Imad's cousin was restoring mosaics in the monastery, but the figure he had seen wasn't Abu Majid. For the next two minutes,

Imad and the man in the courtyard shouted at one another across the chasm of the Wadi Qelt. The conversation established that Abu Majid had taken the day off, and Imad packed up his telescope.

It had been a pleasant expedition, but it seemed rather pointless, and as we walked back to the jeep, I asked Imad why he had brought me to the Wadi Qelt, rather than the bird-ringing station. He told me that it was one of his favourite places – that he had often walked through it as a child. He was born in Beit Sahour in 1958, to a poor family, and as a boy he had helped his mother grow vegetables to sell to their neighbours. He was also an enthusiastic member of the Boy Scouts, and when he spent a year studying at Bristol Polytechnic in 1982, he went on a pilgrimage to Brownsea Island, the site of the first Boy Scout Jamboree. For many years he worked as a lab technician at Bethlehem University, but he wanted to translate his love of nature into action. In 1992 he set up a non-governmental organization called the Environmental Educational Centre (EEC) in the grounds of a school called Talitha Kumi, in the village of Beit Jala, on the other side of Bethlehem from Beit Sahour. In 1998, he left to establish the PWLS. As well as running the ringing station, the PWLS promotes ecotourism and animal welfare, and soon Imad hopes to establish the first environmental institute in Palestine. Praiseworthy aims, no doubt, though again I found myself wondering what to make of his puzzling arrangements – were they indicative of the way that Palestinian society functions, or merely a product of his own relaxed and haphazard style?

The next day, I visited the ringing station at Talitha Kumi. They had netted a blackcap and two common chiffchaffs before I arrived and at eight a.m. I went round the nets slung between almond trees and fig trees in the school's terraced grounds with Riad Abu Sa'ada, the director of the station. We found a chaffinch and a robin – a bird the Palestinians regard with as much affection as the British do. They call it *abu henna* – 'the father of henna' – because its breast is the colour of the dye used in wedding ceremonies.

Riad freed the birds from the nets, placed them in cloth bags and took them to an open-air platform in the woods, where he weighed and measured them. He held their heads between his fingers as he wrote up the notes, and their beaks moved across the page as though they were taking an intense interest in the recording of their specifications. It was a pleasant morning's work, and yet Beit Jala lies in one of the most contested areas of the West Bank. The settlement of Har Gilo occupies a hilltop three kilometres to the west, and the Jerusalem suburb of Gilo stands on the other side of the valley. During the second intifada, Palestinian militants used to shoot at Gilo from Beit Jala, and the Israeli Army responded with characteristic severity: many houses in the village were destroyed and dozens of people were killed. One morning, Riad and Simon Awad, the executive director of the EEC, were nearly shot by Israeli soldiers when they were taking down the nets by the wall that overlooked the road to Har Gilo.

Riad had finished his assessment of the robin and was holding it with its claws pinned between his fingers and its head upright.

Hunting birds is part of the culture in Palestine and Riad said that people are often surprised when they ring them and release them. 'We just open the hand,' he told me, 'and let it fly away.' It was like a magic trick in reverse – one minute the bird was there, quivering faintly, and then it was gone. *Abu henna* took off in a blur of flickering wings and disappeared into the trees, free to resume its northward migration.

III

Then spake Joshua to the Lord in the day when the Lord delivered up the Amorites before the children of Israel, and he said in the sight of Israel, Sun, stand thou still upon Gibeon; and thou, Moon, in the valley of Ajalon. And the sun stood still, and the moon stayed, until the people had avenged themselves upon their enemies. *Josh.* 10: 12–13

I visited Yossi Leshem's radar station at Latrun on my last day in Israel. I wanted to see it in operation, and I was pleased when Leshem himself offered to show me around. I shouldn't have been surprised: it soon transpired that Leshem manages his PR as assiduously as every other task he undertakes. Weeks before we had met outside a hotel in Jerusalem and he had emailed me a folder of articles detailing the highlights of his career. As we drove down Highway One to Latrun, he kept grabbing a clipboard stowed behind the steering wheel and making notes of other items that he wanted to show me. By the time I left his office, I was equipped with a multimedia presentation of films, articles and photographs documenting his achievements.

Most of it has been concerned with bird migration. Leshem was born in Haifa in 1947, the eldest son of two German Jews who arrived in Palestine in the 1930s, and he was imbued with a love of nature from childhood. His mother wasn't interested in wildlife but she liked hiking, and she used to take her sons into the mountains every week. In 1971, Leshem founded the first bird club in Jerusalem, which Amir Balaban attended as a boy, and for many years he worked for the Society for the Protection of Nature in Israel.

In 1980, he was working on a survey of raptor migration when a pilot suggested they go up in a plane to see if there were more birds aloft than they could count from the ground. Leshem thought it might make a good research project and he went to the air force to request the use of an aircraft. While he was there, they showed him unpublished data on collisions between birds and aircraft: in the previous ten years, five aircraft had been destroyed, and every year at least three planes were seriously damaged.

Soon afterwards, a honey buzzard collided with a $5 million Skyhawk near Hebron and destroyed the plane. The pilot survived only because the bird came through the canopy and hit the ejector handle. The air force agreed to sponsor Leshem's PhD and he started work at Tel Aviv University, where he now teaches a course on bird migration. At first, he hired teams of birdwatchers and used the radar at Ben-Gurion Airport to plot the birds' paths, but he soon realized that there was one crucial detail neither could ascertain – the only way to gauge the height at which the birds were flying was by going up in a plane and flying with them.

Most of the planes he tried were too loud and disruptive, but eventually he settled on a motorized glider that allowed him to fly 'wing tip to wing tip' with the birds. In the next five years, he recorded a total 1,400 hours of flying time as he tracked the main paths of the migration. He established that the birds follow three routes through Israel and the West Bank – if they don't go along the Rift Valley, they cut across the south-west corner through the Elat mountains, or fly parallel to the coast, exploiting the currents created by the offshore winds that are displaced upwards when they hit the slopes of the Judaean Hills.

In 1984, Leshem began producing the maps of the 'bird plague zones' that now hang in the briefing rooms of every squadron during the migration, and once the pilots knew the main routes the birds tend to follow, the collision rates fell dramatically. But the birds didn't always behave as predicted. When Leshem finished his PhD in 1991, the air force asked him to build a radar system designed to supply additional 'real-time information' about their movements.

Leshem's first and most important step was to enlist the help of a former Soviet general, who had emigrated to Israel in 1991 at the height of the mass exodus of Jews from the Soviet Union. Dr Leonid Dinevitch is an expert in weather forecasting, and he used to run a joint civilian–military project employing forty-seven radars and three aircraft that generated artificial rain. Leshem – the inveterate fixer and facilitator – found him a place at Tel Aviv University, and Dinevitch found him a cheap decommissioned radar in Moldova.

'At that time,' Leshem told me, 'if you were connected, you could get anything you wanted.'

When the radar arrived in Israel, Leshem began looking for a place to put it. It didn't take him long to settle on Latrun. It lies in the heart of Israel, halfway between Jerusalem and Tel Aviv, on one of the main routes of the migration. It also occupies a footnote in biblical history and a significant place in the history of modern Israel. The Ayalon Valley witnessed a legendary battle during the conquest of Canaan, when God prolonged the day to allow Joshua time to defeat the five Amorite kings, and it was also the site of several important battles during the War of Independence. When British rule in Palestine ended on May 15, 1948, the police fortress they had built at Latrun was left in the control of the Transjordanian Arab Legion.

David Ben-Gurion, the prime minister of the state of Israel, which had come into existence the day before, believed it was essential to control the road to Jerusalem, and during the next two months, he ordered repeated attempts to capture Latrun. Ariel Sheinerman – later Ariel Sharon – was injured in the first assault, and the second and third were among the first occasions that the Israeli Army deployed tanks and armour. None of them succeeded – Latrun remained under Arab control until the Six Day War in 1967, when Israel defeated the armies of Egypt, Syria and Jordan and pushed back its de facto borders by occupying the West Bank and Gaza. For fifteen years, the strategic fortress at Latrun was no more than a stopping-off point on Highway One, but in 1982 the Armored Corps recognized its place in its importance by converting it into a 'memorial museum', Yad La'Shiryon, which now attracts 400,000 visitors a year.

Leshem had decided that he wanted to combine his radar with a 'living museum' documenting the coexistence of birds and aircraft, but he knew the migration alone wouldn't generate the kind of audiences he wanted and so he approached the general of the Armored Corps. 'You are telling the story of the bloodshed, the heritage, the conflict,' he said. He is a big man with a mop of curley, grey hair, and he talks in a deep, hoarse voice, constantly discarding and revising his words as he searches for the right one. 'This is the story of the past. And I am coming with the story of the future: bird migration, environment, high-tech, radar, Internet, satellites. Give me a piece of land, about eight acres, on your site, and I will build a museum, an auditorium and a scientific centre.'

We arrived at Latrun at eight in the morning, and as we drove round the edge of the museum grounds, we could see the radar, framed between the jutting gun barrel of the tanks that surround the fortress. It stands on the lip of the amphitheatre that the Armored Corps uses for presentations, and from a distance, the dark green metal ball looked like a giant fungus that had flowered unexpectedly overnight. The soldier at the gate waved us through, and as we drew up beneath the radar, Dinevitch appeared, apparently from nowhere, holding a metal board.

Exhibit one, in Leshem's whistle-stop guide to Latrun, was an image of the radar at the height of the migration. The screen's concentric rings were overlaid by a livid green splash running across the centre of the country, parallel to the coast. It marked the presence of a flock – 120 kilometres long – of migrating storks. Exhibit two demonstrated the threat they posed – Leshem had collected fragments of an F-15 Falcon destroyed over the Negev Desert in 1995 in a collision with three storks, and mounted them on the side of the radar itself.

Dinevitch had gone inside the hut attached to the radar and we followed him up. It was like stepping into the interior of a submarine: it was very dark and the walls were obscured with grey metal consoles and banks of dials and switches. A generator hummed in the background. Dinevitch was sitting silently in front of a monitor that translates the machine's analogue signal into digital form.

For the time being, the screen was showing dark blue dots, indicating local birds, but Dinevitch called up a screen with a picture of the autumn migration – flocks of birds moving south on a bearing of 176 degrees, at an average velocity of 56.9 kilometres per hour. While another screen displayed the vertical distribution – most of the birds were below 1,000 metres, and only one or two were above 2,000 – Leshem stood behind me, reciting the radar's triumphs. It has been so successful that the air force bought another for the Negev and another for the north and estimates that the system has saved $660 million worth of equipment, as well as the lives of several pilots.

Leshem adds that it has also saved thousands of birds, and made a minor contribution to regional cooperation: the information is relayed to the Royal Jordanian Air Force, and when it went into operation in 1997, Leshem and Imad Atrash developed schemes encouraging Palestinian and Israeli children to track the migration together.

The project was abandoned during the second intifada, but Leshem's plans for Latrun have continued to develop. He has already built an educational centre with classrooms and dormitories for 244 people on the far side of the museum and he is building a $3 million visitor centre on the empty land beyond the radar. Visitors to Yad La'Shiryon will be able to watch the migration via satellite and, for seven months of the year, to look out for the birds passing overhead. Leshem also plans to turn the woods on the edge of the museum grounds into a bird sanctuary. It will be similar to the JBO, though like everything in Yossi Leshem's world, it will be much bigger and better. 'The site of Amir is one acre. This will be sixty acres. So it will be sixty times bigger.'

Amir Balaban wouldn't have been surprised to have heard Leshem celebrating his defeat with such conspicuous glee. Leshem's unselfconscious egotism makes him seem ridiculous at times, and yet it's part of his undeniable charm and vigour. It was ten to nine and he had to get to Tel Aviv to start work – the two hours he had devoted to showing me Latrun were a prelude to his normal day. We had ten minutes to look round Yad La'Shiryon, and as I trailed around in Leshem's wake, attempting to keep up with his rapid commentary, I found myself wondering about its real purpose. A wall listing the names of the 4,855 soldiers of the Armored Corps who have died in Israel's many wars flanks the courtyard outside the bullet-scarred fortress, and yet the tone of dignified mourning seemed at odds with the presence of the great metal war machines drawn up around the building. Leshem informed me, with his characteristic emphasis on scale, that only Fort Knox has a bigger collection of tanks, and I couldn't decide whether Yad La'Shiryon was a shrine to the dead, or a place devoted to the worship of the martial spirit.

The significance of Leshem's Cold War radar and museum is even harder to understand.

'It's a strange combination, tanks and birds,' he acknowledged as we got back into the car. 'But believe me, it's a big story for the Middle East.'

In his company, it's almost possible to believe that nothing else matters and yet I wasn't sure what to make of Latrun. Leshem has found a way of asserting the importance of the migratory birds that travel over Israel and the West Bank twice a year, and done valuable work to protect them. Does it matter that he had to harness the power of the Israeli Air Force and exploit the centrality of the army in the public's affections in order to do so? Maybe not. Yet I couldn't stop thinking about Sami's project. The separation barrier is the product of Israel's determination to subdue every aspect of its environment in the name of security, and so is Leshem's radar. Nothing, it seems, escapes the militarized nature of life in Israel – even the birds who traverse its skies fall within the invisible net of its security's apparatus. ■

'Macfarlane's prose is as robust as the landscape he describes. Anyone who loves language will take pleasure in this book'
Sara Wheeler

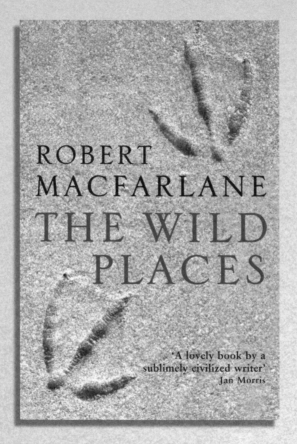

ROBERT
MACFARLANE
THE
WILD
PLACES

'A lovely book by a sublimely civilized writer'
Jan Morris

'A beautifully modulated call from the wild' Will Self

'Rich, sinewy prose to set on the shelf alongside works by Roger Deakin, Richard Mabey, Tim Robinson' **Iain Sinclair**

PAPERBACK EDITION, SUMMER 2008

GRANTA

www.granta.com

GRANTA

THE MAGAZINE OF NEW WRITING

If you enjoy good writing, you'll love Granta – fiction, reportage, memoir, biography and photography four times a year

Subscribe to *Granta* or buy an annual subscription for a friend and receive, with our compliments, a *Granta* special-edition **MOLESKINE**® notebook

Subscribe online at **www.granta.com** or by **Freephone 0500 004 033** or fill in the **coupon overleaf** and send to us

'With each new issue, Granta *enhances its reputation for presenting, in unequalled range and depth, the best contemporary writers in journalism and fiction.*' SUNDAY TIMES

Subscription offer: take out an annual subscription to *Granta* and receive a complimentary *Granta* special edition **MOLESKINE**® notebook

TEAR ALONG PERFORATION TO REMOVE

YOUR ADDRESS FOR DELIVERY

Your address:

TITLE: INITIAL: SURNAME:

ADDRESS:

POSTCODE:

TELEPHONE:

EMAIL:

Billing address if different:

TITLE: INITIAL: SURNAME:

ADDRESS:

POSTCODE:

TELEPHONE: EMAIL:

NUMBER OF SUBSCRIPTIONS	DELIVERY REGION	PRICE	SAVINGS	DIRECT DEBIT PRICES	SAVINGS
☐	UK	£29.95	32%	**£24.95**	**43%**
☐	Europe	£35.95	18%	**£32.95**	**29%**
☐	Rest of World	£39.95	10%	**£35.95**	**18%**

I would like my subscription to start from: All prices include delivery

☐ the current issue   ☐ the next issue   GRANTA IS PUBLISHED QUARTERLY

PAYMENT DETAILS

☐ I enclose a cheque payable to '*Granta*' for £_____ for ____ subscriptions to *Granta*

☐ Please debit my ☐ MASTERCARD ☐ VISA ☐ AMEX for £_____ for ____ subscriptions

NUMBER ☐☐☐☐ ☐☐☐☐ ☐☐☐☐ ☐☐☐☐   SECURITY CODE ☐☐☐

EXPIRY DATE ☐☐ / ☐☐   SIGNED _____   DATE _____

Instruction to your Bank or building society to pay Direct Debit   ● DIRECT Debit

TO THE MANAGER:

(BANK OR BUILDING SOCIETY NAME)

ADDRESS: BANK/BUILDING SOCIETY ACCOUNT NUMBER

☐☐☐☐☐☐☐☐

POSTCODE: SORT CODE

ACCOUNT IN NAME(S) OF: ☐☐ ☐☐ ☐☐

SIGNED: DATE:

Instructions to your Bank or building society Please pay Granta Publications Direct Debits from the account detailed on this instruction subject to the safeguards assured by the Direct Debit Guarantee. I understand that this instruction may remain with Granta and, if so, details will be passed electronically to my Bank/ building society.

Banks and building societies may not accept Direct Debit instructions from some types of account

ORIGINATOR'S IDENTIFICATION

9 1 3 1 3 3

☐ Please tick this box if you would like to receive special offers from *Granta*
☐ Please tick this box if you would like to receive offers from organizations selected by *Granta*

Please return this form to: **Granta Subscriptions, PO Box 2068, Bushey, Herts, WD23 3ZF, UK, call Freephone 0500 004 033** or go to **www.granta.com**

Please quote the following promotion code when ordering online: GBIUK102

DEMOLISHING THE MAZE

WORK IN PROGRESS

Donovan Wylie

The Maze prison was opened in 1976 at the height of the conflict in Northern Ireland between British security forces and Republican and Loyalist paramilitaries. Its function was to contain and isolate political prisoners who had been detained without trial after the introduction of special powers in 1971 and treat them as ordinary criminals. In this way the Maze was devised as an architectural solution to an armed conflict. Its demolition is a testimony to its failure.

I first visited the Maze late in 2002, a year after all the prisoners had been released as part of the Good Friday peace agreement. At that time the prison was still functional, in so far as it was empty but not closed, kept ready for use should the need arise. It symbolized a limbo period in Northern Ireland: potentially the end of thirty years of conflict, but just as possibly the beginning of a new one.

In its construction, the Maze was an architectural version of a Russian doll: a small enclosed space encased by a slightly larger one, then that encased by another, then another and another, eventually covering an area of almost 360 acres, surrounded by a perimeter wall over two-and-a-half miles long. To experience the Maze was to experience a journey of constant, relentless repetition on a vast scale, resulting in a feeling of total disorientation. This was exactly what it was designed to do to those within it.

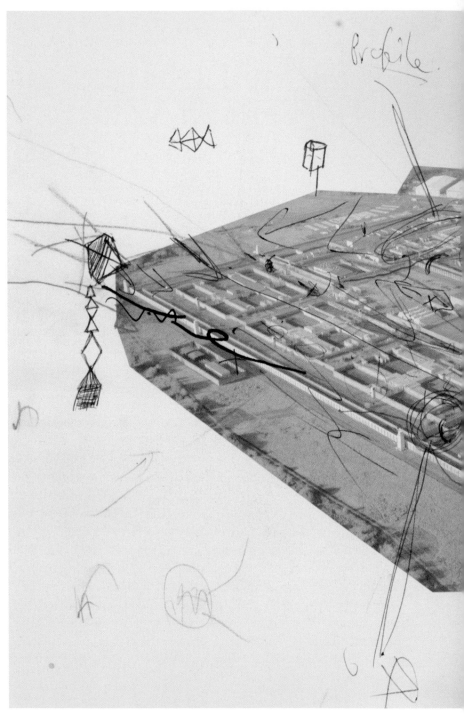

From Donovan Wylie's notebooks: an aerial view of the Maze prison, 2002

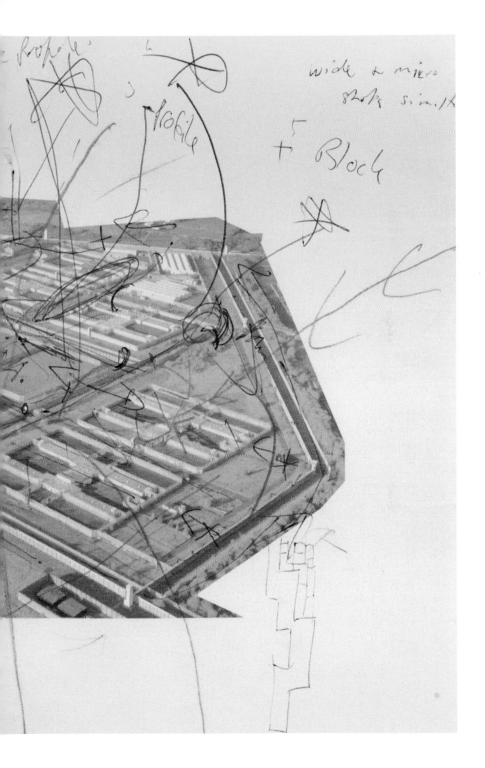

19.   12/07.   Demog H4.

20.   1/08.   Internal walls 2.

21.   1/08.   Internal walls cont.
                    H5 fencing . H3 demol.
                    H5 Internal fencing.
                    H3 Rubble

22.   2/08   H3 . Demol cont.
                    H5 . Internal fencing cont
                    H3 Rubble cont.
                    H5. Remeke fencing.
                    Republican mural.

23.   2/08   H5, Internal fencing
                    piled . H5 Cleared.
                    Chapel Intact.
                    Demog Pics.
                    Internal walls, Foundation
                    Rubble.

In many ways the prison became for me a fascinating object: I spent months, years, photographing it and understanding its every detail and function. I was partly in awe of this human mantrap, and I cannot deny feeling emotional on the first day of demolition and then feeling guilty for this emotion.

The demolition of the Maze is seen as a hugely important symbol of peace in Northern Ireland. Even though the future of the site remains uncertain, its erasure is nothing less than remarkable. The demolition began in spring 2007 and is scheduled for completion by the end of 2008. In its early stages it was more a dismantling than a demolition. Rather than tearing down the fencing, the bolts holding it in place were removed one by one in a process similar to taking apart a massive Meccano set. To remove the fencing around H-Block 2 (the first block to be demolished) took twenty-three days.

Even in its destruction, the systematic nature of the building still persists. Layer after layer of fencing is folded and piled neatly, then delicately carried away. The crushing machine, 'the muncher' (designed to the specifications of the head of a tyrannosaurus rex), gnaws through the internal walls and prison cells. The rubble is then sifted to separate out the reinforced steel entwined in the concrete, and the purged concrete is heaped in the centre of the prison, slowly growing to the size of a small mountain. All the rubble will be recycled as hard core, and used for future building on the site, a kind of political morphology.

Destroying a building such as the Maze is mind-numbingly tedious. One member of the demolition team told me that he couldn't sleep at night for the relentlessness of his days' work. As a photographer, trying to make visual sense of this project has felt equally relentless. I have spent 130 days at the Maze this year. The task is gruelling, and the solitary nature of the work is having personal repercussions. As each layer falls there is the sense of getting closer to something, and the falling of each layer has become, for me, a moment to contemplate why all of this happened. But the further one penetrates, the less seems to be revealed, as if there are no answers at all. ∎

The Maze site, 1986, showing its eight H-blocks and the former Long Kesh internment camp

Clarke explosion

↓

Open water

Wall + rubble to
Phase 3.

Concentrate on
* block rubble* both sides and
all of them same in clearance.
This is main task from here on,
after final stage of fencing.

* Idea of rubble lies alone

an wall fergs ;   1.35.4 line → racets Rd. 3.

- stages of internal fencing : → wings.
1) fencing. 2/ fencing pulled down. 3/ fe

st. 4. Inner.

one.
stage 2.
(1st layer off).

inner
stage 2.

inner.
st. 2.

Pulled out. 4) fencing bundled up. 5) Bare block & posts.

St. 2. outr.

outr
St. 2.

outer
stage
3

inner –
(block beginning
demol.)
inner or
St. 4.

CHERRY TREE GARDEN

A rural stronghold in the South Bronx

Matthew Power

I grew up in the Champlain Valley of Vermont, in a draughty old clapboard farmhouse. Through the coldest months, we supplemented oil heat with a cast-iron wood stove, burning cord after cord of seasoned hardwood. So it is curious that I never learned to split wood or handle an axe until I went to the South Bronx.

Our farmhouse was on an apple orchard: a mile deep of McIntosh, Cortland, Red Delicious, Northern Spies, marching in neat rows towards the Adirondacks in the west. Across the road, a meadow subsided into a hardwood swamp running uninterrupted to the banks of Otter Creek, two miles east. Bread Loaf Mountain rose above and by October was often dusted with snow, the first intimation of winter. Growing up there was a strange and solitary idyll, governed by the moods of seasons and weather and family, the smells of mud and manure and mown hay and wood smoke. Long before my parents divorced, or the house was sold, or the orchard was razed for feed corn, this landscape instilled in me a sense of impermanence.

In the summer of 1997, at the age of twenty-two, I washed up in New York City, and promptly fell in love with a beautiful and fiercely independent punk girl named Amy, with a shaved head and an inextinguishable spark of adventure. She seemed to me to embody all the anarchic joy and freewheeling possibility the city offered the young and broke; a muse of dumpsters and bicycles, game for anything. The city was all strange, and all new to be discovered, and I followed her down its rabbit holes.

One hot July afternoon she took me on the '6' train up the length of Manhattan, beneath the mud of the Harlem River, and we climbed at last out into the brightness of Mott Haven, a neighbourhood in the southernmost reaches of the South Bronx. We were on 138th Street, with its yellow and red bodega awnings, and in their shade old Dominican men sitting on milk crates, playing dominoes, drinking Colt 45 from paper bags with straws. We rounded a corner, and for the first time I saw the pre-war apartment building called Casa del Sol rising in the summer shimmer like a mirage. The broken-windowed, graffiti-tagged, five-storey tenement occupied most of its block. A jagged crack ran down its facade, creating a fault-line between the bricks, and a helical length of razor wire strung over the rusted metal gate had snagged a bounty of plastic bags and unwound audiotape, which floated on the breeze.

A large orange highway sign, the block letters rearranged, read: THIS IS OUR COMMUNITY. CLEAN UP AFTER YOUR DOG. PREVENT FASCISM. It was the work of Harry Bubbins, one of a handful of people who lived in the building and ran it as a community centre and ad hoc revolutionary base. Harry introduced himself, a tall, handsome man with broad shoulders and a broader smile, a deep laugh and a wild glimmer in his eyes. He wore overalls with no shirt, home-made sandals composed of tyre treads held on with bicycle inner tubes, and a cap with a feather poked into it. He was also carrying an axe. I liked him immediately, despite his tendency to speak in riddles and never answer a question straight. Rafael Bueno, a forty-seven-year-old Dominican man with a corona of frizzy black hair and a silver-toothed grin, worked in the garden, singing unselfconsciously aloud in a thick Spanish accent. Harry's and Bueno's eccentricities were readily apparent, but they seemed to have it together enough to run the place.

We had come up to volunteer, painting signs for a protest against Mayor Giuliani's plan to auction off a community centre in the East Village. As Harry framed it, in the struggle for space in the city, these far-flung outposts had to support one another, and unsanctioned spaces – gardens, squats, community centres – must be fought for, by any means necessary. (At the auction, someone would smuggle in and release 10,000 live crickets, bought from a science supply company, nearly causing a stampede.) We set to work making banners with brushes and cloth spread on the sidewalk. There was smoke, and the smell of oregano and garlic frying over a cook fire in the garden, and curious neighbourhood kids from the projects across the street came over to watch us.

Casa del Sol, or just Casa as we came to call it, sat on a large triangular lot at 136th Street and Cypress Avenue. The tenement, half boarded up, filled half the triangle, while a wild and tangled garden called the Cherry Tree spread over the rest: maple, birch, apple, pear and one namesake cherry tree. Riots of tomatillos and raspberries and roses swarmed over the footpaths and fences, and in midsummer sunflowers stood high as basketball hoops. A few dusty chickens scratched around in the dirt. Cornstalks twined with morning glory brushed the chain-link. Casa's mailing address was on 136th Street, but it had been a very long time since any representative of the Postal Service had come by. The building was bounded on one side by a city bus lot; a second side faced the curving domino row of the twenty-storey Mill Brook Housing Projects, while over the lot's long hypotenuse loomed the raised concrete lanes of the Bruckner Expressway. As an object lesson in the failures of late twentieth-century urban planning, this little triangle in the South Bronx was close to perfection.

asa was a 'Robert Moses orphan', left standing alone when, in the late 1950s, New York City's authoritarian master planner had cut the neighbourhood in half with the Bruckner Expressway. Moses, who headed several key city agencies for over thirty years, was the most influential shaper of New York's landscape in the twentieth century. His construction of a network of expressways was central to his vision of urban renewal and the Bruckner was part of a plan to pump a steady supply of suburbanites into the heart of Manhattan. The result was a crushing rebuke to urban density and mass transit (by a man who never even learned to drive). The neighbourhoods that were bypassed and bisected went into rapid decline, leading in turn to 'blockbusting' (shady realtors using racial fears to scare white people into selling on the cheap), 'white flight' to the suburbs, absentee landlords and a pulling back of services after New York's near-bankruptcy in the mid-1970s.

The sharp drop in property values also contributed to the arson epidemic of the 1970s. Landlords could claim insurance on property that was no longer worth the price of upkeep by simply burning it down. In the late 1970s, there were 7,000 fires in a two-year period, and during the blackout and subsequent riots in the summer of 1977, more than 1,000 fires were counted burning across the city in a single night. Whole blocks were left as burnt-out shells. The population of Mott Haven dropped by 57 per cent in under a decade. So many buildings were destroyed that the nearby 41st Precinct police station changed its Wild West moniker from Fort Apache to the Little House on the Prairie. Huge sections of the South Bronx had ceased to exist as an urban landscape. And then, in the late 1980s, crack arrived in the neighbourhood. By 1990, there were six murders a day across the city.

It was a long decline from the neighbourhood's hopeful origins. Lewis Morris, one of the signatories of the Declaration of Independence, owned vast tracts of what is now the South Bronx. His family's estate, Morrisania, was razed by the British during the Revolution but later reconstructed; Morris offered the land in 1790 to establish the young nation's capital, but Philadelphia beat out the Bronx. He now lies buried in St Ann's churchyard, five blocks from Casa del Sol.

A century after Morris the subways were built, and the Bronx received a wave of European immigrants fleeing the crowded tenements of the Lower East Side. But in the years after the Second World War the automobile and the expressways enabled them to live in the new suburbs, further from the core of the city. Bypassed and abandoned, the South Bronx was left to die. When Ronald Reagan visited in 1980, and used the mountains of rubble as a backdrop to decry the 'broken promises' of the Carter administration, he compared the neighbourhood to London during the Blitz.

Somehow, through the years of arson and decay, Casa del Sol had remained standing. The vacant lot adjacent was planted with trees and tended as a garden. One of the very few rays of light to pierce the long decades of collapse in the city's poorest precincts was the birth of the community gardens movement. Many thousands of buildings, gutted by fire or left to rot, had been bulldozed: the city owned them through tax defaults, but couldn't afford repairs and maintenance. Unattended lots became dumping grounds for burnt cars, broken appliances, all the sea-wrack of poverty. But in neighbourhoods across the city, local residents cleared out the lots, planting trees, flowers and vegetables and creating green spaces in places that government and landlords had left for dead. By the mid-1990s there were more than 700 community gardens, with names such as Green Oasis and Le Petit Versailles and Esperanza – Spanish for 'hope'. And there was the Cherry Tree Garden, next to Casa del Sol, stretching up through the seasons, visible to cars passing on the expressway only as a flash of green beside another bombed-out South Bronx tenement.

Seen from above, after taking off from LaGuardia Airport, Casa del Sol and its triangular lot, surrounded by the flow of traffic heading towards the Triborough Bridge, appeared as though they were being drawn into the tangled vasculature of the city itself, like a blood clot dislodged from an arterial wall. But if you stood in the shade of the little copse of white birches that grew at the sharpest point of the triangle, with the traffic roaring on the expressway above and the rumbling of buses in the city lot, the building resembled a ship, the garden its prow slicing through the sargassum of post-industrial civilization. Early colonizers – milkweed, mullein, sumac – forced their way through the surrounding crumbling concrete sidewalks. Out of rooftops and clogged drainspouts, and up through piles of tyres, *Ailanthus altissima*, the Tree of Heaven (less formally known as the 'ghetto palm'), was establishing itself with the astonishing persistence and ingenuity of the illegal immigrant.

While nature had managed to emerge from beneath the rubble around Casa, by the 1980s the building itself was falling apart. The landlord vanished, taxes went unpaid, the city gained possession and twenty-two families found themselves squatting in their own apartments. In 1997, after years of ignoring the building, the city issued an eviction notice. Harry and Bueno tried to organize the tenants and even went so far as to distribute flyers in the neighbouring projects warning residents to arm themselves against an imminent government invasion. With Giuliani now in charge, the city's response was overzealous. The eviction incorporated not only scores of police in riot gear, but a police helicopter and an armoured battering ram. Everyone was dragged out and the building was boarded up.

But not for long. Within a few months Harry, Bueno and several others had broken in, taking over the building. Bueno and Harry wanted to manifest their wildest fantasies for the space, now emptied of people. One apartment became a kitchen and offices, another an art gallery. There was a library, workshops, and a huge 'ceremonial space' on the top floor. A theatre was carved out of the basement. Only a handful of people lived there, and most of the huge building sat empty, haunted by feral cats and filled with the abandoned possessions of former occupants. Wind blew through broken windows and pigeons nested in empty kitchen cabinets. The police didn't come back, but they knew the building had been reoccupied and eviction was always a looming threat.

That's when Amy and I discovered the place. After that first afternoon, we started coming up to Casa weekly, working in the garden, or helping cook, over a wood fire, the huge meals that were served every Saturday to whoever came from the neighbourhood. Bueno would bring a large hand-crank grinder and feed garlic and oregano and salt into it until they formed a greenish-black paste. This was *adobo*, the key spice in Latino cookery. Fried in corn oil over a fire, its smell could draw you in from a block away, as we made enormous pots of rice and beans and vegetables picked from the garden beds.

Harry had acquired a canoe from somewhere and we took it out on the East River. We paddled in the swirling currents out of Hell Gate, past the razor wire of Rikers Island, the world's largest penal colony, with 15,000 prisoners. Past the roofless, vine-swallowed sanatorium on North Brother Island, where Typhoid Mary had been kept, and where the steamer *General Slocum* had grounded and burned in 1904. Until September 11, 2001 the *Slocum* had been the worst disaster in New York's history, over a 1,000 people drowned or burned to death. Up the Bronx River, lined at its mouth with mountains of scrap metal for recycling, giant cranes shrieked on the bank as they dropped loads of shredded steel into barges. And yet, in the middle of this rusting industrial wasteland, where the river seemed a forgotten channel running behind abandoned factories and warehouses: a wetland of cattails, a mud-turtle slipping from a log, a snowy egret perched on a shopping cart that sunk into the black mud of the riverbank.

As the fall progressed and the weather grew colder, I would spend long hours in the small lot behind the building, splitting wood. Casa had no electricity, save a single extension cord that ran through the garden and was spliced into the base of a street light, pirating enough current to run a few lamps, maybe a computer. For heat there were several ingenious stoves cobbled out of oil barrels. Harry had put the word out to landscape contractors that we wanted wood and they were more than happy to oblige, rather than pay to haul a dead tree to the dump. Trucks would back up to a gate in the chain-link and unload entire trees, cut up into manageable rounds. I had never chopped wood in Vermont, but I fell in love with it in the Bronx. I put together a canvas mailbag of tools: hatchet, axe, maul, splitting wedges, ten-pound sledge. With the precision of a golfer choosing his club, I'd size up each piece and set to work, coaxing the wood into stove-lengths. A wedge tapped into the centre ring of a slab of birch, or pine, or black locust. A few more knocks with the sledge to set it, then heft, aim and swing. The weight of the hammer did the work, driving the steel wedge deep into the wood.

Usually I would split wood alone. Once, a city bus driver pulled to a stop at the kerb, hopped out and asked if he could have a go at it. If it was cold, breath plumed in the air, the Chrysler Building sparkled in the south beyond the highways and bridges, and the work made it warm enough for shirtsleeves. I'd stack piles by the barrel stoves, stoke the fires if they needed it, warmed twice by the wood. I'd listen to the smoke ticking up the chimney pipes that ran out the window to the roof. It was all so simple, but it felt somehow defiant, a sort of civil disobedience to ordinary life and the expectations the city imposes on both vocation and avocation. It felt honest.

The late 1990s signalled a great change in New York City, even in the South Bronx, a place that for decades had epitomized the collapse of inner-city life. The city's murder rate had peaked in 1990 at 2,245. By 1997 it was half that and in 2007 it fell below 500 for the first time since records have been kept. Giuliani, a former prosecutor who took office in 1994, credited his 'broken windows' philosophy of cracking down on small, quality-of-life crimes like graffiti and turnstile-hopping, as well as CompStat, a pioneering statistical method that tracks crimes geographically and helps police focus on hot spots. In fact, an improved economy and shifting demographics had caused crime to drop for three years before Giuliani took office.

As crime dropped and the economy hummed along, the price of property rose, with vacant lots often doubling or tripling in price in the span of a year. Even Mott Haven was changing: a coin-operated *New York Times* box appeared on the corner of 138th Street (Harry always made sure to leave it jammed open for whoever came along next). Any piece of land within the five boroughs, even land that had been forsaken for half a century, was suddenly a hot commodity. The gardens had been created by local initiative and were arguably a key part of the civic spirit and aesthetic appeal that were reviving the city's fortunes. But the city government had owned the ground beneath the gardens since the taxes stopped being paid decades before. All the same, it was a shock when, in late 1998, the mayor's office announced a plan to raise revenue by liquidating the city's inventory of vacant land. The gardens would be sold to the highest bidder, bulldozed to alleviate the city's housing shortage and bring in revenue. The first auction would be in May, and 115 gardens from across the city would be on the block. We got hold of a copy of the auction book and discovered that the Cherry Tree Garden was on the list.

Casa del Sol became the organizational headquarters of a multi-pronged campaign to stop the auctions. The prongs were: a) legal strategy; b) media outreach; and c) direct action. Seeing as we lacked most of the resources for a) and b), our plans were heavily weighted on c), hoping we could pull off enough theatrics to bring attention to the cause and put political pressure on Giuliani. Gardeners, squatters, community activists and organizers from across the city gathered every weekend to strategize and hold training sessions in civil disobedience and non-violent resistance. It was a wide-ranging group, from teenage anarchists to an eighty-five-year-old woman named Françoise who had fought with the French Resistance. I was, I suppose, radicalized by circumstance, having never even heard of activism before coming to New York, but I loved it.

Giuliani played brilliantly to type, a melodrama's stock villain lacking only a handlebar moustache and top hat. In that era before September 11, before he became America's Mayor, he had spent much of his mayoralty in the exercise of petty tyrannies. We were only the latest addition to his catalogue of bullying, following squeegee men, the homeless, squatters, cab drivers, ferret fanciers, jaywalkers, fare beaters, sidewalk artists and elephant-dung portraitists of the Virgin Mary. A popular sticker of the day portrayed Giuliani with devil horns, vampire fangs and a Hitler moustache. Overkill, granted. But they were exciting times and all of us were possessed with a revolutionary fervour. Giuliani accused us of being 'stuck in the era of communism'. But what he failed to understand was that he had given us moral clarity and a sense of real purpose.

Citing security concerns, Giuliani had severely restricted access to City Hall, but in February we were allowed in for a public hearing on the fate of the gardens in the City Council chamber. The futility of public hearings in New York City is an open secret – they are held merely to say that they were held – but we flocked in to testify anyway, many of us clad in insect- flower- or vegetable-themed costumes. At a prearranged signal, a large group stood up and filed out of the chamber to stage a sit-in on City Hall's front steps. A plain-clothes policeman blocked the door in a panicky spread eagle, so we decided that the sit-in was going to happen right there, and sat. We started singing 'This Land is Your Land' at the top of our lungs, disorderly voices echoing in the building's huge ornate rotunda. Several dozen police with helmets and batons piled into the hall, but none of us put up a fight. Going limp, we were put in flex-cuffs and dragged by our armpits to waiting paddy wagons. Thirty of us were locked up overnight in Central Booking, below the streets of Chinatown. I got a migraine under the buzzing fluorescent lights, but it was still the most fun I'd ever had.

Back at Casa, we had found the entire contents of a Puerto Rican prom rental shop left behind in one of the abandoned apartments.

All thirty of us went to our formal appearance in court dressed in a rainbow of shiny, ruffled tuxedos. And so it went on, through the winter and into the spring, a steady stream of demonstrations, stunts, street performances, near-riots, mass arrests. And we kept pushing harder. Public support, which was always on the side of the gardens, appeared to be making Giuliani cast about for a face-saving solution. On the last day of April, a dozen of us gathered in a park at the foot of the Brooklyn Bridge. The auction was only five days away and we had decided that I was going to climb a tree outside City Hall, dressed as a sunflower, and not come down until Giuliani came out and spoke to me.

I crossed the street and stood, casually as I could, at the corner of the park. There was a policeman only thirty feet away, directing traffic at the intersection. I half expected him to run and tackle me the moment I touched the tree. But suddenly he left the intersection and walked around the corner, out of sight. So up I went. The first branch was about seven feet high and after a brief scramble where I thought I was too shaky to climb, I made it. Looking back at the street corner, I realized nobody had even noticed. So I went higher and higher, my face brushing against the new ginkgo leaves.

I took the sunflower out of my pack, unfolded it and put it on. I'd made it myself, from yellow satin stretched over bent coat hangers, an old belt and lots of duct tape: a huge golden corona of petals, with a hole for my face sticking in the middle. And still no one looked up. My friends had all congregated at the bottom of the tree, and began holding up their signs and chanting, calling on Giuliani to stop the auction.

He didn't appear. As it turns out, he wasn't there, though I had no way of knowing that at the time. Nobody seemed to be paying much attention to our brilliantly orchestrated plan. Finally, a lone cop on a scooter pulled up, looked at me and shook his head. He asked if I wanted to come down. I said no thanks. He replied they were going to lock me up. I said they'd have to come get me first. Aside from the setting, it was a fairly typical New York City impasse.

A crowd started to form on the corner. Reporters and cops shouted questions at me, and I shouted back. But somehow, despite all the noise and commotion below, I was in an envelope of stillness. I could see an inchworm crawling on a branch nearby. A light breeze off the East River shook the leaves on all the trees, and I could feel myself swaying. Birds flitted from the stop light to the branches, and then dropped to the ground to peck for crumbs. It seemed, up there, that this was really the whole point of trying to save community gardens, that in a city with so little open space for so many, the gardens allowed some of the feeling of calm I felt up in that tree. In the tree I was free and down on the ground I would not be.

Four emergency services vehicles screeched up, one a truck with a boat on the roof, apparently in case I tried to catapult myself into the East River to escape. There were about thirty police under the tree and a dozen reporters. A huge airbag was inflated beneath me, of the sort placed below window ledges for would-be suicides. A ladder was placed against one of the lower branches. I climbed a little higher. There wasn't much tree left. An emergency services officer in jumpsuit, hard hat, heavy gloves and climbing gear ascended the ladder. I was still another dozen feet above its top. He began to climb, nervously, clipping his harness to each flimsy branch. I asked him whether he climbed trees very often. No, he was a bridge man. Jumpers.

I didn't want him to feel compelled to yank me down, so I decided to negotiate. We shook hands. He said he understood why we were doing this, but he had to do his job. I didn't want to trouble him over it. So he descended and I followed, stopping at the top of the ladder to straighten my petals before climbing to the ground. I had a vague sense of handcuffs snapping around my wrists, of flashes bursting in my face and a television camera thrust at me as I was stuffed into a waiting police van.

With the day of the auction fast approaching, the city, in a last-minute deal, negotiated with two non-profit open space groups to buy the gardens for over $4 million. Bette Midler was involved in the deal and the negotiations had been conducted in secrecy. It wasn't what we'd hoped or intended, but perhaps the end result of our radicalism was to make negotiations with mainstream groups more palatable to Giuliani. On one hand, this set a terrible precedent: the city had held public space hostage, and although they sold it to a buyer who would preserve it, they still sold it. On the other hand, all 115 gardens that were to be auctioned would be preserved in perpetuity. Amy and I would say that over and over to each other: preserved in perpetuity.

The Cherry Tree Garden was saved, but work at Casa del Sol continued. And naturally there were other battles to be taken up – and mostly lost. There was the eviction of Dos Blocos, a squatted tenement on 9th Street in Manhattan, which was welded shut and barricaded from the inside, the roof lined with long metal spikes to fend off cranes. Or CHARAS, an East Village community centre, sold to a developer. Or Esperanza, the garden on 7th Street, whose defenders constructed a Volkswagen-sized frog filled with concrete. Bulldozed, and replaced with one of the anonymous mirrored-glass condominium towers, $1,500 a square foot, that have popped up around lower Manhattan like glittering toadstools over the last decade.

But the South Bronx, even by 1999, was still somewhat immune to the development craze beginning to sweep Manhattan and Brooklyn. Junkies would still come to the block to snort quick dime bags of heroin; the blue glassine bags littered the sidewalk. Hookers would conduct business negotiations with taxi drivers. Stolen cars would be abandoned on the block and often set ablaze. One warm August night, while Harry and I were buying beer and avocados at a deli on the corner of Cypress, we heard a loud series of pops outside. We ran out to find a young Hispanic man lying in a pool of blood on the sidewalk. While Harry called 911, I held his hand, which was cold, and talked to him quietly, telling him the firemen were coming from down the block, that he was going to be okay. The next day I found out from a detective that he'd died on the way to the hospital. When I asked if they had any leads on who was responsible, he quipped world-wearily: 'nobody saw anything, yet'.

The summer after the sale of the gardens, Amy and I moved into Casa. We took an apartment below Harry's, full to the ceiling with junk. I spent days carrying old furniture, stained mattresses, refrigerators and stoves down four flights of stairs. The entire skeleton of a cat rattled out of a couch and shattered on the floor. The windows were stapled plastic sheets and diesel soot from the Bruckner Expressway covered everything. We tried hard to live there. We lit candles. We bathed with water heated on the stove. The roof leaked and we spent days carrying buckets of hot tar up and patching it ourselves. Amy painted our room bright blue with yellow trim, and if we piled on enough blankets we could get through an autumn night without freezing.

In the autumn, we cleared an area in the middle of the garden and set up a canvas teepee. Its top reached nearly as high as the roadbed of the Bruckner and cars would sometimes slow to peer over the edge at the incongruous sight. Harry invited a friend of his, a Navajo medicine man and Vietnam veteran, to conduct a peyote ceremony the night before Thanksgiving. We sat up all night around a fire, huddled under blankets, trying our best to focus on the bitter medicine and pray through to the dawn. I don't know that I believe in the ability of a psychoactive plant to cleanse the doors of perception, but staying awake all night, caught between the dampness of the earth and the warmth of the fire, the city outside seemed to vanish.

Life at Casa was harder than I'd expected. My relationship with Amy was eroding, compounded by the difficulties of our living situation, but more by my own restlessness and impatience, by some inability to focus on the work that Casa was supposed to be achieving. Pipes froze and burst, the roof leaked; merely keeping the building intact was a full-time job and Bueno expected us to dedicate our lives to his vision for the place. Amy and I argued often, took out our stresses on each other. The revolutionary excitement of the garden fight, the belief that we were changing the world, were hard to maintain in everyday practice.

We lasted about four months. By December, Amy and I moved out and split up not long after. She got an apartment in the neighbourhood with her sister and I spent the winter travelling in Central America. We stayed friends and returned often to visit Casa, but it was never the same again. Harry moved out a year or so later, and by 2004 Bueno was the only one living in the building. When the Republican National Convention came to New York, he threw open the doors to protesters from all over the country, and hosted almost a hundred punk kids and young anarchists who hoped to shut down the convention. Over 1,000 were arrested, jails overflowed, people were penned for days in a bus garage nicknamed 'Guantanamo on the Hudson'. Some of the kids stayed on at Casa and a few dozen lived there through the fall.

But time finally ran out. The city, which had always owned the tax lien on the building, sold it to an affordable-housing group. In December, the police came and evicted everyone at Casa. Bueno was arrested for refusing to leave. That same day, as they sealed up the building, workers hired by the city turned on the long-dormant electricity and started a fire. The decades-long scourge of the neighbourhood finally came to Casa. By the time the firemen put it out, the top three floors of the building were gutted and part of the roof had collapsed. The exact cause of the fire, coming so soon after the eviction, was mysterious.

I went by Casa del Sol recently, to find the building transformed. The brickwork had been repaired and the long cracks had been sealed. The windows were all replaced and the graffiti and murals blasted away. A security camera pointed at the front entrance. The garden was tended to, but had a chain and lock on the gate. Through a window, in what had been our kitchen, I saw a spotless new apartment. The rest of the neighbourhood is changing too. The *New*

York Times has taken to calling it SoBro, a branding exercise perhaps of overly hopeful realtors. Nevertheless, the tide of gentrification, even in the present housing downturn, continues to lap further and further outward. Manhattan now is lost to all but the rich and the luckily rent-controlled. The irony is starker there, where the gardens we saved are surrounded by shiny new glass-and-steel condos. Has the city changed too much, fallen too far under the sway of money, for anything as strange and magical as Casa del Sol to return to existence? Was that time in the South Bronx just a moment at the far ebb of some historical tide, when the land was most exposed and we thought we could claim it for our own? Or do those tides of gain and loss, controlled by some unseen economic gravity, pulse back and forth forever?

When I contemplate the answers to those questions, I recall riding my bike, at sunset in winter, over the Willis Avenue Bridge and into the South Bronx. The long dusky light silhouetted the blocks and spires of Manhattan and cast long shadows as I looked down into the Harlem River rail yards. The scene was desolate: weeds grew up between the sleepers and staghorn sumac wove itself through chain-link and razor wire. From between a string of rusting boxcars, a pair of ring-necked pheasants strutted across the barren rail yard, elegant tail feathers trailing along behind, gorgeous even in the fading light. The two birds were immigrants, an introduced species made wild again by chance and instinct and necessity. They seemed like exiled regents returning to their kingdom. ■

'Daydreaming has been my making and my undoing'

Roger Deakin

Introduced by Robert Macfarlane

In 1969 Roger Deakin bought the ruined remains of an Elizabethan steading and twelve acres of surrounding meadow in rural Suffolk. Little survived of the original sixteenth-century dwelling except its spring-fed moat and its vast inglenook fireplace. So Roger put a sleeping-bag down in the fireplace, and lived there while he built a house around himself.

Walnut Tree Farm, as he christened it, was made largely of wood. Its frame was of oak, chestnut and ash, and more than 300 beams supported its roof and floors. Roger kept the doors and the windows open all year round, in order to let air and creatures (swallows, spiders, bats) circulate. The house seemed almost to breathe. At its back was the moat, in which he bathed regularly. Over the decades, Roger also towed various structures into his fields, including a shepherd's hut in which he fitted a bed and a stove, an old wooden caravan, and a railway wagon. He would often sleep or write in one of these 'satellites', as he called them.

Roger died of cancer on August 19, 2006. At sixty-three, he was far too young for death. Over the last six years of his life, he kept a journal of a kind: a record of his travels, his thoughts, his reading, but above all of daily life at Walnut Tree Farm. He filled forty-five notebooks with his distinctively bold but scrawly handwriting. During these notebook-years, Roger was researching a book called *Wildwood*, about the vital role that trees still play in our lives and our imaginations. Like D. H. Lawrence, he felt wood to be 'the fifth element' of the world. His journals were the place in which he first tested out ideas and images that later emerged in *Wildwood* (which was published a year after his death).

'Much as I enjoy the process of writing and the exercise of my own skill and craft in getting it right,' Roger wrote in one notebook, 'nonetheless I would often prefer to be a jotter. Jottings, in their spontaneity and complete absence of any craft, are often so much truer to what I actually feel or think at a given moment.'

Selected and edited by Alison Hastie and Terence Blacker, the following entries are taken from a larger extract of Roger's diaries arranged to form one composite year. Some abbreviations have been amended, but otherwise Roger's words have been left to speak for themselves. ■

MAY

I have a lost ant on my desk. It has been there for several days, wandering about in a baffled sort of way, I catch glimpses of it as it ducks out of the shadow of a coffee mug and dives under the overhang of my writing pad. Then it decides to make a break for it across five inches of open desk and shelter under my glasses case. But it's a restless soul, and no sooner has it arrived under the deep strip of shadow under the glasses case than its off again, this time to the haven of an old copy of 'Sight and Sound' where, to my surprise, instead of burrowing under, it marches straight across an interview with the film director Monte Hellman about Two Lane Blacktop, pausing on a picture of Dennis Wilson, James Taylor and Laurie Bird standing on a rock looking into a river. But this ant is never still. It's off again already, running along between the tramlines of grain in my Oregon pine desktop and disappearing under the blackness of the telephone. How does it survive? What is the secret of its never-ending energy?

I can't help it with directions, because I've no idea where it came from in the first place. I could make a guess and simply put it outside. But it is cold and rainy out there; not ant-weather at all, so it is better off in here, although I worry that I may accidentally squash it under a book, or under my elbow.

It is like a Palestinian, evicted from the Gaza strip. It is a refugee from somewhere, frantic to go home, cut off from its family and fellow workers, going mad with loneliness. I suppose if I'm honest, I feel some fellow feeling for it myself, cut off in book-purdah, while my friends are out there at play.

The knowledge that this tiny creature is lurking somewhere on my desk, but could be anywhere, means that I daren't move anything in case of causing an accident to it. Where is its home? What keeps it

...for 'free' copy.

...se – a lean-to woodshed:

'up' The Sparrow Hawk meant as a book.

~~Sparrow Hawk~~ ~~Kestrel~~ : Died 6th August 2001 (Monday)
10am outside the kitchen door. Probably kamikaze divebombed onto the drainpipe and killed itself on impact. It has been feeding on left-over cat food on their box outside door – swooped by a cat. No blood – warm & supple when I found it.

Weight: 5oz/4oz. 1 foot exactly.
Length to tip of tail: ½ inch long.
Talons: 1½ ins long. 4 very sharp hooked claws, each 1cm long. (¾")
Beak.

Dark brown on back feathers edged in orange/russ white & brown s around head & chin breast.

life size Tail 5 ins long

12 tail feathers underneath brown

going all this time? Will it run out of energy? Should I feed it honey as one would feed a bumblebee?

Cut off from its tribe, it has lost all sense of itself. It is really a part of a body in search of the rest of the body, like the tail of a lizard, left twitching after amputation. An ant-colony is really a single organism, differentiated into the various functions, chiefly feeding and breeding, so if each one tiny component gets lost like this, it feels some imperative, some compulsion, to rejoin the rest of the ant body.

I feel sorry for it, but I suppose there's nothing much I can do for it. Just when I think I'll never see it again up it pops, doodling its imaginary trail all over my desk. If I could somehow get it to walk through ink and trace its path, it might make some sense, some pattern even, but I doubt it. It is just a wandering ant, a damned soul, condemned to eternal exile on my desk, like Philoctetes. The kind of ant you get in your pants. One of the few ants in the world whose natural enemy, the human, is actually concerned about its survival as an individual, except that the concept of individuality is completely alien to an ant.

*

Why write? A writer needs a strong passion to change things, not just to reflect or report them as they are. Mine is to promote a feeling for the importance of trees through a greater understanding of them, so that people don't just think of 'trees', as they mostly do now, but of each individual tree, and each kind of tree.

Look at Richard Flanagan and his strong political campaign against Forestry Tasmania and its destruction of the old-growth forests. He has very publicly withdrawn from the literary prize sponsored by Forestry Tasmania, and he has even produced car stickers attacking the use of poison to kill marsupial animals in newly-felled forests.

JUNE

I slept in the shepherd's hut last night after an 8 length evening swim in the moat, now beginning to weed up, and a beautiful nearlyfull moonlit night. Very bright, hardly proper darkness at all. At ten to four I was woken up by a warbler (not sure which) hopping along the tin roof of the hut, then striking up most beautiful song, at first utterly solo in the half-light, soon joined by other birds. It sang its heart out, moving about the roof now and again between phrases or cadenzas to a new vantage point. Easing myself up on one elbow about twenty past four I inched back the curtain and surveyed the field. Yellow pools of buttercups, and here and there a pyramidal orchid, and even a lovely lush marsh orchid in intense purple and a huge stack of a flower like a wedding cake.

A crow was flying in big circles about the field, climbing steeply now and then, then gliding down, as if for pure pleasure. I dozed back to sleep but was awoken by a most terrific rumbling and shaking of the whole hut, and a scratching sound. I thought a cat must somehow have leapt in through an open window and onto my bed. But I think it was the roe deer, the one with the fawn, rubbing against the hut, as I heard what sounded like hooves disappearing through the long grass. The birdsong now far too raucous for sleep, so I adjourned to the house over dewy grass for breakfast, and to wrap a leaving present for Frank Gooderham, my lovely postman.

I found myself in tears as I wrote his card and wrote in the copy of my book I gave him, and as I wrapped the present: a bottle of Graham's port, a book and audiotape, and my card. I hadn't fully realised, until that point, how deeply important he has been to me, working and living here alone for so long, and looking forward each morning to the cheering flash of his red van through the trees, tuning my ears for the hum of its Ford engine as it approached and changed gear along the common and down my bumpy track.

*

I got up at 4.30am and went over to Wortham Long Green to look for orchids etc, and especially the Dyer's Greenwood. Couldn't find this at all, following Richard [Mabey]'s directions that it was at the far end of the green, but I did find yellow bedstraw (Ladies) and the white heath bedstraw, and knapweed, self-heel and a marsh orchid. Oxeye daisies too.

In other parts I found marjoram, meadow cranesbill in verge, two or three feral cardoons, forget-me-not, a big stand of dozens of marsh orchids at the other end, near the T junction, bee orchids next to more marsh orchids, hay rattle at the end near tennis courts and house 'For Sale' sign, hoary ragwort, and the gnarled old pollarded trunk of the black poplar, still just about alive with a single surviving branch. I have seen others on this common deliberately set on fire up their hollow trunks, acting as chimneys.

I went down to Redgrave Church on its hill above the cornfields and stumbled upon the grave of Julie Ward. It was a shock, realising I was standing before the grave of a young woman who had been murdered in 1994 (10th October) in the Kenyan bush, her body mutilated and half-burnt and her murderer relentlessly pursued by her grieving father, outraged at Kenyan corruption and laziness.

Julie Ward was a talented photographer and had taken some fine pictures on her African travels. It is obvious from the photographs that she was courageous and adventurous. The simple square headstone bore an engraving of a hippopotamus above her name. The animal stands on the savannah plains of Kenya, with a few sparse trees in the background. I hadn't expected to find a hippo amongst the rabbits and moles of Redgrave churchyard. But why Redgrave? It was good to think that the young woman had been buried here in this beautiful, isolated place, overlooking the African-looking bleached cornfields from high up.

*

Midsummer Day. The perfect morning for it. Wood pigeons cooing in the young elms and ashes surrounding the garden in deep shadow. Spider's gossamer threads glinting in the sunshine. Robins on the lawn. There's a goat-beard head stuck in a jam jar swivelling in the breeze at the open window of my study. An earwig explores the window frame, and an ichneumon fly elegantly strolls up and down the window pane. A distant cockerel across the field and even the neighbour's distant barking dogs, or Michael's crop-scorer across the common sound benign this morning.

Yesterday I stood by the front pond and watched a carp slowly emerging from the black depths, rising imperceptibly by slow degrees until I could see its face, and its eyes, and its great gaping, gulping, mouth, and then, as it caught the sun, its golden scales. I calculated that it must be at least 25 or even 30 years old and was one of the fish Barry Day deftly caught in his digger bucket when he was removing the silt from the moat fifteen or 18 years ago.

A willow warbler sings in the spinney by the old goat-sheds. Bumblebee workers, all from same colony, gather pollen and nectar from the new deep crimson flowers of the water figwort. Great 3 and 4ft spires of elegant little flowers of the most amazing deep crimson. I record them, and the post van arriving too.

*

At about 5pm I go out and begin scything the cowparsley in the garden outside my study facing the common. Its flowering is over and it is going to seed. I need a new scythe blade really, but they're getting harder to find. I shall buy one in Chagford next time I'm on Dartmoor.

Working with a scythe is silent, rhythmical, and conducive to thinking. A power tool simply jams the brain solid with its din and violence and sense of hurry. A scythe is unhurried, but it can fell a fair-sized area of grass and herbs in an hour of steady work, and by six I have very nearly cleared the whole front lawn.

Now I fetch the pitchfork and rake all the cut cowparsley and long grass into compact heaps and carry each one to a bigger haycock in the middle of the lawn. As it grows higher in a cottage-loaf shape it becomes springier, and bounces a little each time a new load is dropped on the top. It will soon settle, especially when it begins to heat up inside and compost.

This is my idea: to make a pile of the cut stems on the lawn and let it compost down, thus reducing its weight and bulk to something more managcable for eventual carting to the vegetable garden.

As I work all the robins in the neighbourhood gather on the cut grass and begin feeding and hunting for flies. Then both cats come and sit in the new-mown hay, observing the robins with feigned indifference. All of them are following deep instincts, attracted by the smell of the hay, the sounds of me working, and the smells of fresh-cut herbs.

On my daily bike ride later on, I had stopped outside Gislingham, opposite a small wood and a pile of blue cartridge shells, to satisfy my curiosity about an unlikely plant community growing along a high field bank where the road has become a Holloway on the descent into Gislingham. The ditch was dug much deeper along here two or three years ago and the fields were drained.

Growing in the ditch and on the bank are: fool's watercress, water figwort, tufted vetch, common yellow vetchling, cornflowers, whose seed must have already been in the ground, meadowsweet.

I was sitting on my bike admiring all this when I heard the rumble of hooves thundering lightly up the road in my direction. I looked round and there was a pair of roe deer galloping straight up the middle of the road towards me. They saw me, and veered off into the cornfields, one bounding off one way, the other off to the far side of the road. Both were hinds, and probably had fawns hidden up somewhere, perhaps in the shooting wood. Deer move through fields of corn like dolphins through the sea.

*

Tomatoes on toast was about the only thing my father knew how to cook and when my mum was away we would eat the dish for breakfast and dinner too, with toast and dripping for lunch. I used to love arranging the halved grilled tomatoes on the toast like jelly fish.

*

Cats are as Norman O Brown calls in Life Against Death, 'polymorphously perverse'. That is to say they are gloriously alive in every part of their body and get equal pleasure from the stimulation of any part of it, free of what Brown calls 'the tyranny of the genitals'.

This morning Alphonse lies on the bare earth outside the front of the house full length on his back, stretching and rolling from side to side or raising all four legs into the air and just lying on his back. He purrs to himself and gives that cat-smile by narrowing his eyes when he looks across at me.

*

With plants and trees in woods abroad – in, say, Kyrgyzstan – I had the feeling you get when you're in a late night bus, say, and you encounter a group of friends you don't know at all – total strangers

– and feel you would like to know them, feel some immediate sense of kinship, that they are 'your sort'. It is like falling in love with a whole group of people at once.

Later, once you've got to know them by talking, you introduce yourselves (c.f. Kavanagh's poem – 'We fell in love long before we were introduced'.) And it is love.

I can't bear to mow my lawn because it would mean mowing all the blueness out of it, the vanishing blues of self-heal, bugle and germander speedwell. They are worth more to me than the neatness of a mown lawn, although, in truth, I have loathed neatness ever since school, and uniform, and collars and ties, and haircuts.

A gentle tinkling as the lantern brushes against the ball grass-tops on my way across the hay meadow to the railway wagon at midnight. The dancing shadows in the grass. The deeper darkness inside the wagon.

JULY

When I was 17 years old a policeman came to the door and told me my father had died that afternoon. He had been found dead in a tube train at Euston Square Station. He had a heart attack on a tube train. That might actually have been the moment that made me into a conservationist. When I was writing poems like 'Gentian' and later on fighting for Cowpasture Lane, I was wanting back what I had lost. I wanted my father back. I didn't want to lose anything more. I had lost such a big part of my life, I needed to compensate by holding on tightly to everything else.

*

People ask how a writer connects with the land. The answer is through work. Look at John Clare, working on the land, knowing it by working on it and being in it for years from earliest childhood. Look at Alice Oswald, working as a gardener for six years, living in Devon, and not owning a car, so she walks and bicycles everywhere. Look at Ted Hughes or Henry Williamson, both farming and living with animals.

And when we work on the land, what is our connection with it? Tools, and especially hand tools. You can learn much about the land from the seat of a tractor, the older and more exposed the better, but to observe the detail, you must work with hand tools.

*

In my cabin I learnt the sheer luxury of daydreaming. It has been my making and my undoing too. How many days, weeks, months have I lost to it? But perhaps it isn't lost time at all, but the most valuable thing I could have done. ∎

MEMOIR

COLORADO

Benjamin Kunkel

Of all the boxy western states, Colorado and Wyoming are the boxiest – almost perfect rectangles – and when I was a kid and wanted an idea of my state I could do no better than to picture a box of Neapolitan ice cream. Just as a block of such ice cream is divided into three equal portions of strawberry, chocolate and vanilla, Colorado consists of a high semi-arid plateau in the western third of the state; the heaped summits of the southern Rockies in the centre; and in the east the plains rolling away towards Kansas. It's mostly the mountainous central part of the state, however, that people have in mind when they think of the place, and as it happens it was there in the real *Coloradan* part of Colorado that I grew up. At first we lived in a cabin my parents had built up Salt Creek, outside of the town of Eagle, with the help of other long-haired recent transplants – it was part of that movement of hippies 'back to the land'. And once I was of an age to walk around the world unattended, I don't believe I had any trouble understanding why my parents had been drawn to this land in particular, or why adults should pronounce the word

'Colorado' with a certain inflection of romance and pride.

The mountain to one side of Salt Creek fanned up in sheets of sun-scoured red sandstone dotted with piñon and juniper trees; sometimes, in a patch of overlapping snow and shadow, you saw a cactus too. The mountain opposite was a different world entirely, since it faced north and conserved its water in the shade: a sombre looming mass thick with spruce and fir. The first of the beautiful ordinary things I remember are the creek gabbling away in its bed and the smell of rained-on sage bringing out an unsuspected sweetness from the land: thoughts of water in a dry place. But the thinness and dryness of the air on clear days – as of something brittle that would never break – was also thrilling, and what I liked doing on days like that was to clamber up the red mountain, which always offered some new place to be discovered among its troughs of brilliant dirt and tilted spines.

Jean Stafford, probably the best writer Colorado has so far produced, described the state's atmosphere better than anyone in her short story 'The Mountain Day': 'The violent violet peaks stood out against a sky of cruel, infuriated blue, and the snows at timberline shone like sun-struck mirrors.' In the same story, a red canoe gleams 'in the pure light like a bright, immaculate wound'. I don't know why this language of hurt should attach to alpine Colorado, or why, in the best-known version of the traditional song, the man of constant sorrow ('I seen trouble all my days') should be bound for Colorado ('where I was born and partly raised'). Unless I do know why: the pure light and gin-clear air can't be matched by your life. They will only put a hurt look into your eyes, whether you stay or go.

Not that nowhere else in America has clear light and thin air – but unlike other such places Colorado isn't frigidly cold, or bone dry, and most of its tall mountains aren't even overwhelming. The peaks of the southern Rockies generally start from so high a base that they don't tower away from you; their summits are almost companionable, in spite of their location in the sky. This means that alpine Colorado doesn't repel or begrudge habitation in the way of most alpine places; and faces of red sandstone flood many a cold valley with a fictitious sensation of warmth. The warmth can be quite real, too, in a state as far south as Virginia, at least until the sun passes behind a cloud and leaves the air, with no memory for scent, moisture or temperature, as cold as if the sun had never shone.

The combination of thin air and thick geology is instruction in the brevity and virtual unreality of our own time, and must supply the reason why so many schools of American Buddhists have established centres and retreats here. Of course the shopping centres strung along the highways and the stack-a-shack condos (as I remember my father calling them, when they first appeared in the Eagle Valley) propose their own lesson in non-attachment, being so recently built beneath durable mountains, and never built to last.

For as long as I can remember I have had a sense of the shallowness and impermanence of American settlement in Colorado. My father comes from Oregon, my mother from Massachusetts, and they met as undergraduates at the University of Colorado, where my father had gone on a skiing scholarship and my mother gone, I think, because she, unlike her siblings, didn't want to become a banker or remain a Catholic. They settled up Salt Creek in 1971 and my father's parents followed them there. My parents' friends were amateur bee-keepers, gardeners, cabinetmakers, guitarists, and our more immediate neighbours likewise seemed to be making things up as they went along. One had a field full of junk cars, many children and a drinking problem; he was always driving off the road. Another ran the local airfield and kept a mountain lion for a pet; when he and his wife divorced later on, she married an arms dealer and moved to Istanbul.

There was nothing else I knew – we didn't have a TV – but even so I could tell our life was new and rare and unsponsored by tradition. Perhaps I sensed how far from north-shore Massachusetts my mother felt, living in a narrow mountain valley and raising three kids in a cabin heated by a stove. Everything was improvisation, with the thrill and risk the word implies. My father the former English major, with no training as a land surveyor, started a surveying company when he and his partner both chipped in twenty dollars to open a bank account. And life up Salt Creek acquired a real enough frontier air on at least those occasions when a pack rat ventured out from the wall in the living room and my father picked up his .22 rifle to shoot it, a practice that could be unsettling to guests but which mostly impressed me as a display of good aim. No doubt precisely because we lived eight miles from town, and the town of Eagle was so rudimentary in those days, my parents didn't want us to grow up uncivilized, and not only insisted that we wear trousers to the dinner table but drilled us there in good manners.

I never thought we would stay up Salt Creek forever. It was plainly in the nature of mountain valleys, with their grey abandoned barns and garden plots being reabsorbed into the land, that you left them one day. And yet when we moved away to the enormous metropolis of Glenwood Springs (pop. 5,000), I felt the loss of my red mountain more intensely, it seems, than any loss since.

G lenwood Springs is named for the natural hot springs that emerge, smelling of sulphur, near the junction of the Colorado and the Roaring Fork rivers, and as a spa town centred around a huge outdoor pool Glenwood has always attracted more than its share of quacks and people in need of a cure. In 1887, this meant that the gunfighter Doc Holliday repaired to Glenwood when he fell ill with TB; his grave is a local landmark. In Willa Cather's *A Lost Lady*, a visit to the town revives for a time the failing spirits of lovely, tragic Mrs Forrester: 'Last winter I was with the Dalzells at Glenwood Springs for three weeks,' she says, 'and I was surprised at myself. I could dance all night and not feel tired.' From the early 1980s, I recall a high incidence of New Age religion, born-again Christianity, health kicks, diet fads, even spoon-bending. My mother went no further in the direction of Reagan-era self-reinvention than to get a perm and begin doing aerobics, though her connections in the exercise world meant that when the movie *Breakin'* (1984) caused me and some friends to develop a mania for break-dancing, she was able to recruit a dance teacher from the community college to give us pale mountain children classes in moonwalking, head-spinning and the worm.

Along with the religious fashions and lifestyle improvisations of the adult world, there were also divorces and bankruptcies, and when one of the partners with whom my father had invested in real estate went bankrupt and needed some cash, our family returned to Eagle to take up residence in the vacation house the man had built while he was flush. Our own finances were all right because my father had started a software company in Eagle, of all places; he'd learned to fly a small plane and this enabled him to deal with clients throughout the West. In the fields just below our new house we kept horses and experimented for a time with grazing cattle. My mother began teaching aerobics herself. And when I admired my parents, it was for their adaptability to new circumstances, and when I disapproved of them it was essentially for the same reason: I told myself they didn't know what they were doing.

It may have been that I set about convincing them to let me go back East to boarding school because I had the notion that somewhere in America people did things more or less correctly and by the book. And at school in New Hampshire I did meet kids from places like New England, the South, even California, where evidently there existed more in the way of traditions and customs than we had in Eagle. These people and their parents knew or pretended to know how to speak and dress, possessed a common store of cultural knowledge, often observed the rites of some religion and vacationed in the same places year after year. It took me some time to grasp the source of all this assurance: these families also belonged to a far more clearly articulated class structure than mine had in Colorado. Then I began to miss the Western indifference, if not to money, then at least to status and prestige. I was far from indifferent to those things myself, and feeling that it sounded better to come from Colorado in general rather than Eagle in particular, 'Colorado' became where I said I was from, with the result that after enough repetitions of this claim I was able to convince myself that I really was somehow derived from the state at large.

Culturally, economically and historically, the western plateau and the eastern plains don't have much in common, and even the mountainous middle section of the state is literally split in two by the continental divide. If such a territory existed in Europe or Asia, the people on the western slope of the mountains would speak one language and the people on the eastern slope another; in South America, they'd at least fly different flags. Even in the western United States, where borders are mostly ruler-straight, the north–south state lines (since North America is a continent of north–south mountain chains) often fall roughly alongside the spine of the mountains. None of Colorado's borders, however, corresponds to any natural fact, so that, even more than other states, Colorado has to secure its existence mostly in the mind.

It's as difficult to say what the idea of the state is as to deny its existence, though certainly it has something to do with beauty, purity and independence. To every Coloradan I know, in any case, that romantic place name 'Colorado' signifies much more than simply that the first Spanish missionaries noticed the red colour of a big river flush with spring run-off. Two in particular of the Spanish also noticed, one evening, while lost in a spring blizzard – or so the legend goes – that the high mountain looming before them was impressed with a cruciform snowfield starkly distinct from the surrounding face of rock, a snowfield so miraculously centred on the north-east face of the peak and so proportional to the cross of the Roman Church that the lost Spaniards can hardly be blamed for taking this glimpse of what is still called the Mount of the Holy Cross for a sign that their journey was blessed; and perhaps contemporary Coloradans can likewise be forgiven for loading a mere administrative rectangle with romantic ideas.

Colorado gains many more residents than it loses every year, especially in and around the cities along the Front Range, at the base of the Rockies, and it would seem that especially since the late 1960s, when the image of California began to darken, Colorado has taken on some of California's role as an American promised land of natural beauty, affordable real estate and a brand-new chance.

Severance from history is probably the deepest tradition of the place. I was nineteen before I knew to ascribe the thinness of the human presence on the land to the fact that Colorado had rid itself more completely of Indians than any other western state or territory: no small distinction. Today in all the large extent of Colorado – eighth biggest of the states – there is only the slightest sliver of a reservation and Indians, in my childhood, were not the real if marginal presence they are in New Mexico, Arizona or Montana. My idea of the state – it is still the prevailing idea – was a slide-show succession of prospectors, cattlemen, downhill skiers: romantic individualists. I didn't know that the tin-pan prospectors had been swiftly replaced by gigantic concerns like the Colorado Fuel & Iron Company, property of the Rockefellers. The coal strike called against this company by the United Mine Workers in September 1913 came to a head on April 20 of the next year when the National Guard machine-gunned an encampment of striking workers and their families, killing seventeen people, ten of them children: a scandal that ninety years ago would have been the best-known political fact about Colorado. I never heard of the Ludlow Massacre while growing up. The state to this day remains an open shop.

People think of early Coloradans as rugged Protestants lighting out for the territory and forget the earlier career of this idea. By 1924 the Ku Klux Klan dominated both parties in the state house; the governor was a Klansman and so was one senator. With relatively few blacks or Jews to persecute, the Klan directed its energies against Catholics and Orthodox Christians – those Italians, Mexicans, Greeks and Serbs who formed the largest portion of the organized working class. And this would seem to be the ugly side of that feeling of purity the mountain air can inspire – that such a beautiful place is especially vulnerable to being spoiled by the presence of the wrong people.

In the 150 years since the Pikes Peak gold rush, people have come to Colorado to be among the first ones here. They have settled, by the millions, along the Front Range in order to be alone with nature and with others of their kind. Today at the foot of Pikes Peak spreads the agglomeration of strip malls and suburbs known as Colorado Springs, North American headquarters of both the Christian Right and (in the suburb of Manitou Springs) the New Age witchcraft movement. And this is only the beginning of the enclave character promoted by the mountains. Besides Buddhists, Wiccans, hippies and evangelicals, there are also communities consecrated to winter sports and to Mormonism. But what the geography of the mountains really fosters, in present-day America, is a translation of class stratification into literal terms of altitude. The rich live at high altitude, where they enjoy unobstructed views of snow-covered peaks, the cleanly green glitter of aspen trees, and what F. Scott Fitzgerald (adjusted for inflation) called the consoling proximity of multi-millionaires. With every hundred-foot drop in elevation, property values decline, along with the moisture content of the soil, until a valley has broadened out into a semi-arid scrubland where workers in the so-called service industry plant their trailers among the sagebrush and low tan hills.

A few years ago, when my parents found that the Eagle Valley had filled up with housing developments and shopping centres, they moved away to the South Fork of the White River, up against the Flat Tops Wilderness and twenty-two miles from the nearest town of Meeker. So they went back to the land a second time, now with a satellite TV and Internet subscription. My father put in a landing strip at the bottom of the driveway. My mother, who had seemed like such a sociable person, turned out to be satisfied writing emails to her friends and far-flung children, and taking long hikes with my father and their dogs. And the hikes you can take on the South Fork are truly something, with deer and elk, foxes, ermine and pheasants, and even the occasional black bear or mountain lion slipping through the stands of spruce and aspen and ponderosa pine, while the blank sound of the river unfurls itself continuously in the distance below.

We forget that before the nineteenth century mountains were not what they are today: they were wild waste places, difficult when not impossible to live on or to cultivate, and they weren't considered beautiful. In the days before, say, the Louisiana Purchase (in which Jefferson acquired for the United States a corner of what's now Colorado), if an ordinary American were asked to explain why some places on earth were mountains and others were not, he would probably have replied, in line with the physico-theology of the day, that such inhospitable land must have been cursed or simply abandoned by God. And even if he didn't believe in such explanations, the cultural hangover from them would have prevented him from regarding mountain landscapes as picturesque. It took romanticism in philosophy and the arts, with its creed of individual spiritual growth and its love of wildness and solitude, to bring about a revaluation of mountains. Then their barrenness became their purity, and their quality of abandonment a symbol of spiritual independence – a fundamental shift in perception that at length became the second nature of the ordinary person, especially once supplemented by a geological understanding of how mountains form. Today not even the fundamentalists of Colorado Springs ascribe the existence of mountains to eruptions of God's temper.

Colorado has been one of America's proving grounds of romantic individualism, and lately has come to illustrate the contradictions of romanticism as a mass phenomenon. The contradictions are inevitable when everyone seeks seclusion in the same pristine spots: there goes their seclusion and pristineness. So you move on to another valley, and renew the process you have just fled, or you remain in your large house on its small lawn of scorched grass, and resent your neighbours for spoiling your view as you spoil theirs. In theory, it would be possible to build dense townships and small cities in the mountains, thus concentrating in one place a population that is after all united, if in anything, by its attraction to intact landscapes. In practice, even a still-small town like Eagle is an amorphous spill of suburbs and commercial parks spreading out from a disused old downtown. And that, too, might be fine – everyone might consider sprawl perfectly fine – if most Coloradans didn't still long for the old uncluttered land, and feel that it was everyone but themselves and their like-minded friends who was a blight on the face of nature.

The other contradiction of mass romanticism in Colorado comes from the geology of the state itself: coal, natural gas and oil shale, all of which Colorado has in great abundance. There in the mountains my parents have created the happiest picture of married life in one's sixties that I know, but by the time I reach their age I doubt whether oil will be so plentiful and cheap that it will be possible to fly a small plane from a landing strip at the bottom of your driveway, or drive twenty or forty or sixty miles to go shopping. And if these things do remain possible, it may be because Colorado's Piceance Basin and Colorado's Roan Plateau have been so intensively mined and drilled for their respective reserves of oil shale and natural gas that the area will be unrecognizable. The land Coloradans cherish, land they came for or have stayed for, will turn out to have been loved not wisely but too well, as the burning of fossil fuels generally spells the end of a stable climate (perhaps including a stable ski season), and provokes a series of droughts that a dry part of the country with a population growing by almost two per cent a year would seem unlikely to endure with special grace. It's hard to predict what will happen to Colorado, and to the country from which it is hardly divided by its set of perpendicular lines, but it seems clear enough by now that you can't have a population of many millions pursuing a lifestyle devoted to seclusion, mobility and the picturesque without undermining those same things. Already that cruciform snowfield first seen as a Roman cross by the pair of lost Spanish missionaries tends to melt away and disappear for longer and longer portions of each year. ∎

LAND'S END

In the footsteps of J. T. Blight

Philip Marsden

S ome years ago, in a second-hand bookshop in Falmouth, I discovered a book by the Cornish artist and archaeologist J.T. Blight. As a young man in the 1850s and '60s, he had explored Penwith, the western-most region of Cornwall and had written with unusual fervour about the rare birds and flora he discovered there, the spectacular coastal scenery, the folklore and history, the churches and wayside crosses and the strange collection of megalithic chamber tombs and stone circles that can be found on the region's moors. He completed several books, exquisitely illustrated with his own engravings. As a writer, painter or academic, he could have made his name far beyond his hometown of Penzance, but today he is little known. In his mid-thirties, while engaged with what should have been his greatest book, his career was abruptly ended.

No other landscape I know is so haunting, so suggestive of other worlds, as west Penwith. The ancient stone structures on the treeless moors, the granite cliffs, the abiding sense of extremity – all this combines to suggest some eternal, unsolved riddle. For centuries archaeologists and mystics, geomancers and anthropologists have speculated about Penwith's ancient stone structures, without conclusively explaining why they were built or who built them. Blight himself, who spent more time on their study than anyone before or since, plunged into the mysteries of the stones and never came out. He once quipped, in one of his lighter moments, 'What a delightful lot the ancients were to construct so many puzzles for the moderns.'

Recently, there has been a modest revival in Blight and his work. A biography has been locally published in Cornwall and some of his paintings have been turned out of Penzance attics; a couple of his notebooks have also reappeared. For most of his life, Blight lived in Morrab Place in Penzance, close to the Morrab Library where he undertook so much of his studying. In the basement of the library his sketchbooks and papers are stored in tissue-lined boxes. Having read the new biography, I spent a couple of days at the library looking through the archive and reading his various self-published books. I was impressed once again by his gifts as an artist and by his diligence as an archaeologist, his sensitivity to place and landscape.

One recent overcast morning, I walked out along the cliffs of Penwith's southern shore. For hours I saw no living creature but birds. My gaze was drawn constantly from the path to the sea. A smoky ceiling of cloud was shifting above it, pierced by sunlight. It was here that Blight developed his wonder for the natural world. He had a fascination for the shapes of the rock and for the caves and fissures of the undercliff. His later work on the ancient sites, with all their unsettling questions, grew out of carefree days on this stretch of coast.

I headed inland, to the north and east, and climbed out of a steep-sided valley and on to the moor. The wind struck me at once. I turned slowly through 360 degrees: the sea stretched out to the north, the bald hills to the west, the Lizard Peninsula burrowed away far to the hazy south, the bulk of Cornwall widened to the east. I walked westwards. Broken granite was everywhere, fringing the fields far below, scattered in chips at my feet, raised as menhirs or arranged into stone circles and quoits. In the mid-afternoon I reached Chun

J. T. Blight in 1871

Quoit, the most spectacular of them all. Its sloping capstone stands on a squat stone column, making it look a little like an outsize boletus mushroom.

Blight chose to study Chun and similar chamber tombs for his most ambitious work, *The Cromlechs of Cornwall* ('cromlech' is the Welsh for such tombs). In the Morrab Library, I had read the book, hugely impressive in its range and detail. He took precise measurements, produced plans and drawings. Days of toil went into examining each structure – beginning and ending with an arduous walk from Penzance. But it was not just fieldwork. Blight had spent years reading around the subject of early burial practices. He quotes in many languages, draws on accounts of early burial sites from south Bengal to the Caucasus and uses literary references from the Bible to *Beowulf.*

It is now thought that the Penwith chamber tombs were built at the beginning of the third millennium BC by migrant groups who were probably also the first to strip the land for planting. A recent theory suggests that the monuments may have been erected in imitation of the granite tors, which themselves are believed to have been built by former inhabitants. In this way, the chamber tombs were an attempt, perhaps, to legitimize not only stewardship of the land but also its exploitation. Likewise, Blight and others recorded the local conviction that the quoits and stone circles were the work of an ancestral tribe of giants.

I sat down with my back to the granite. The wind soughed in the grass. Layer upon layer of belief now cover these sites, layers of cosmological speculation. Each generation has projected its own troubled view of the world on to the moors and their stones, and found expression here for its own need to belong – from the Neolithic farmers, to the giant-believers, to the astral visionaries of the New Age. Blight's efforts were part of the same process. In *The Cromlechs of Cornwall* he was, like the original builders of the stones, engaged in the ceaseless human search for life beyond death, for meaning in the flood of time, for a healing of the great rift with the natural world.

The Cromlechs of Cornwall was never published. The Morrab copy is the only one in existence. As he worked on it, through the late 1860s, Blight's moods became more erratic. 'I have a notion of which I cannot get rid that my brain is all wrong,' he confessed. He became increasingly solitary, walking the moors with his sketchbook in hand, his plumb lines and his measuring strings. He had fallen in love with a local woman named Evelina Pidwell. As the daughter of local gentry, she was socially far removed from Blight, the schoolmaster's son. 'In love!' he wrote, underlining the words sixteen times. 'Can't work – frantic.' His infatuation together with his obsessive absorption in work, pushed him towards mental collapse.

He had little encouragement from her, and understood her indifference to be a reaction to his own dismal circumstances. Desperate to raise his status, he tried to start a photographic business, and to sell more of his paintings. He sought wider recognition as an archaeologist by working even harder to complete *The Cromlechs of Cornwall*. The Morrab copy shows how close he came. It is a printer's proof. In the margins, in Blight's own sepia-coloured hand, are his corrections. But the corrections stop before the end, and the last pages are missing. On the morning of May 25, 1871, J.T. Blight stepped aboard a train at Penzance, with a guard on either side of him. A court order had been issued against him: the charge, harassment of Evelina Pidwell. At Bodmin Road station, he was taken from the train and escorted to the gates of St Lawrence's asylum. He was thirty-five years old. He never returned to Penzance, never again saw Evelina Pidwell or the moors of west Penwith.

Thirteen years later, a second edition of one of his earlier books, *Churches of West Cornwall*, included an announcement that its author was now dead and that 'Archaeology has lost not only an enthusiastic fellow student, but a hard worker'. In fact, Blight was still in St Lawrence's and would remain there for another twenty-seven years. He eventually died on January 23, 1911.

The next day I carried on through St Just towards Land's End itself. There was a time when a pilgrimage to Land's End, as to Europe's other Atlantic headlands, was considered a serious and pious undertaking. From the Bronze Age and probably long before, the belief existed that as the sun dropped into the western ocean, it rose on the Isles of the Blessed; witnessing its disappearance in life would ease your later passage there. Many scholars now suggest that this idea is somehow linked to the great concentrations of early tombs in Penwith and on the Isles of Scilly.

In the late afternoon, I crossed the mile-long beach at Sennen and followed a path to the top of the cliffs there. I walked through boulder fields and soft, wind-flattened heath. The sea below was steely-grey, stretching out beyond the Longships rocks. Dusk had fallen when I reached Land's End itself. The buildings of 'The Land's End Experience' were deserted; the wind clattered at a Wall's ice-cream sign. In the cliffs below, I found a narrow gully and climbed down to a grassy ledge. The rock dropped sheer to the surf far beneath me, and I sat to watch the slow darkening of the sky.

One cold day in 1906, when Blight was still at St Lawrence's – elderly now and forgotten – the writer W. H. Hudson visited Land's End. He found many visitors there that afternoon but noticed in particular a scattering of old men sitting on separate rocks, all looking out to sea. Hudson imagined that each one was discovering some visionary faculty lost in early childhood, suddenly able to see where his soul would travel after death. If so, wrote Hudson, he would meet not 'a beautiful blessed land bright with fadeless flowers, nor a great multitude of people in shining garments and garlands who will come down to the shore to welcome him'. Rather, he would need to cross a vast wilderness where the sky is grey-blue and the rocks are grey and the trees are covered in grey-green leaves, a place where there is no birdsong or sound of running water, no wind and rain, a place, above all, of eternal solitude: 'His peace will never be broken by the sight of human face or the sound of human speech, since never by any chance will any wanderer from the world discover him in that illimitable wilderness.' ∎

CONTRIBUTORS

Mark Cocker's seven books include *A Tiger in the Sand* and *Crow Country*, which was shortlisted for the 2008 Samuel Johnson Prize.

Roger Deakin, who died in 2006, was a writer, film-maker and broadcaster and the author of *Waterlog: A Swimmer's Journey Through Britain* and *Wildwood*. His notebooks, *Notes from Walnut Tree Farm* edited by Terence Blacker and Alison Hastie, will be published in October.

Anthony Doerr is the author of a collection of short stories, *The Shell Collector*, a novel, *About Grace*, and a memoir, *Four Seasons in Rome*. He was chosen as one of *Granta*'s Best of Young American Novelists in 2007 and his story 'Procreate, Generate' appeared in that issue.

Paul Farley is the author of three collections of poetry including *The Ice Age*, which was awarded the Whitbread Poetry Award in 2002, and, most recently, *Tramp in Flames*.

Niall Griffiths was born in Liverpool in 1966 but has lived in mid-Wales for over a decade. He has written six novels, most recently *Runt*, numerous short stories, travel pieces and radio plays.

Seamus Heaney's most recent collection of poetry is *District and Circle*. *Stepping Stones*, a book-length interview by Dennis O'Driscoll, will be published later this year. He won the Nobel Prize in Literature in 1995.

David Heatley's work has appeared on the cover of *The New Yorker*, in the *New York Times* and *McSweeney's*. His graphic memoir, *My Brain is Hanging Upside Down*, will be published in October.

Jim Holt writes about science and philosophy for the *New York Times* Magazine. He is the author of *Stop Me If You've Heard This: A History and Philosophy of Jokes*.

Kathleen Jamie's poetry collections include *The Tree House*, which won the Forward Prize in 2004. A book of essays, *Findings*, appeared in 2005. 'Airds Moss' appeared in *Granta* 90.

Benjamin Kunkel's debut novel, *Indecision*, was published in 2005. He is one of the founding editors of *n+1* magazine.

Richard Mabey's books include *Whistling in the Dark, Flora Britannica* and *Beechcombings*. His biography of

Gilbert White won the Whitbread Biography Award in 1986.

Robert Macfarlane's *Mountains of the Mind* won the 2003 *Guardian* First Book Award. He is a Fellow of Emmanuel College, Cambridge and the author, most recently, of *The Wild Places*. He is a contributing writer to *Granta* and wrote 'Blitzed Beijing' for the last issue.

Philip Marsden lives in Cornwall. He is the author of five books, the most recent of which is *The Barefoot Emperor: An Ethiopian Tragedy*, and last appeared in *Granta* 83 with 'The Weather in Mongolia'.

Sean O'Brien was awarded both the T. S. Eliot Prize and Forward Prize for his most recent collection of poetry, *The Drowned Book*, published in 2007.

Justin Partyka was born in Norfolk in 1972. He is working on his first book of photographs, *The East Anglians*. Photographs from this long-term project were featured in the Tate Britain exhibition 'A Picture of Britain' in 2005.

Lydia Peelle's short fiction has appeared in the *O. Henry Prize*

Stories: 2006 and *Best New American Voices: 2007*. Her debut short-story collection will be published in 2009.

Edward Platt's *Leadville* won a Somerset Maugham Award and the John Llewellyn Rhys Prize. He is currently writing a book about the West Bank city of Hebron.

Matthew Power is a contributing editor at *Harper's* and *National Geographic Adventure*.

Jonathan Raban's most recent books are the essay collection, *My Holy War*, and a novel, *Surveillance*. 'Bad Land' appeared in *Granta* 49.

Donovan Wylie was born in Belfast in 1971. He has published several books, including *The Maze* and *British Watchtowers*, and his photo essay 'Out of It' appeared in *Granta* 56. He is working on a new book and a film about the demolition of the Maze.

Contributing Editors
Diana Athill, Jonathan Derbyshire, Simon Gray, Sophie Harrison, Isabel Hilton, Andrew Holgate, Blake Morrison, Philip Oltermann, John Ryle, Sukhdev Sandhu, Lucretia Stewart.

GRANTA | 103

THE ENEMY WITHIN

Inside the British jihad: a remarkable investigation by Richard Watson; **Binyavanga Wainaina** on what it means to be Kenyan after the ravages of ethnic cleansing; **Isabel Hilton** in China and Tibet; **Philip Delves Broughton** on the trail of rogue trader Jérôme Kerviel; **Geoff Dyer** visits *The Lightning Field*.

www.granta.com

Web exclusives: Interviews with **Jonathan Raban**, **Lorrie Moore**, **Robert Macfarlane** and others; Zimbabwean writer **Petina Gappah** on her country in crisis; short films and audio discussions with *Granta* contributors; original fiction by emerging writers in our New Voices series; news, blogs, photography and highlights from the archive, updated daily.

Granta is grateful for permission to quote two lines from 'Birch' by Louis Simpson from *The Owner of the House: New Collected Poems 1940–2001*. Copyright © 2003 by Louis Simpson. Used by permission of BOA Editions, Ltd., www.boaeditions.org; to Random House Group Ltd (UK) and Henry Holt and Company LLC (US) for permission to quote one line from 'Birches' by Robert Frost; to A.P. Watt Ltd (UK) and Simon & Schuster Adult Publishing Group (US) for permission to quote two lines from *The Celtic Twilight* by W. B. Yeats; to the Woody Guthrie Archives for permission to quote from the liner notes of *The Columbia River Collection*; and to The Richmond Organization for permission to quote one line from 'Roll, Columbia, Roll'.